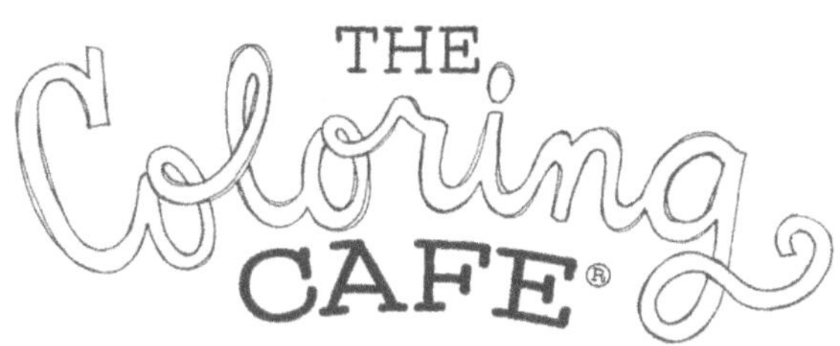

Easy and Simple Beach Fun Large Print Coloring Book

by Ronnie Walter

The Coloring Cafe-Easy and Simple Beach Fun Large Print Coloring Book/Ronnie Walter
ISBN:978-1-7361574-7-3

Welcome to The Coloring Café®!

Hello, Friend!

Who doesn't love a day at the beach? With this coloring book, that day can be today!.

The larger print is great for seniors, those who are just starting to explore this creative outlet, or even for those who need a break from more complicated designs.

I recommend coloring with markers, colored pencils, or even crayons work beautifully on this paper. NOTE: If you use markers, make sure to slip a scrap piece of paper between the pages to keep the ink from bleeding onto the next page.

Remember, coloring should be relaxing and that includes relaxing your expectation for perfection. My drawings are quirky and certainly not perfect, but I love making them. My intention is to provide you an opportunity to find a calm and pleasant moment in your day. So enjoy!

Thank you so much!

Ronnie

P.S. If you'd like to share your work on social media, please use the hashtag #coloringcafe so we can all enjoy your masterpieces!

P.P.S. The last page of this book is a handy space to test your colors!

www.thecoloringcafe.com

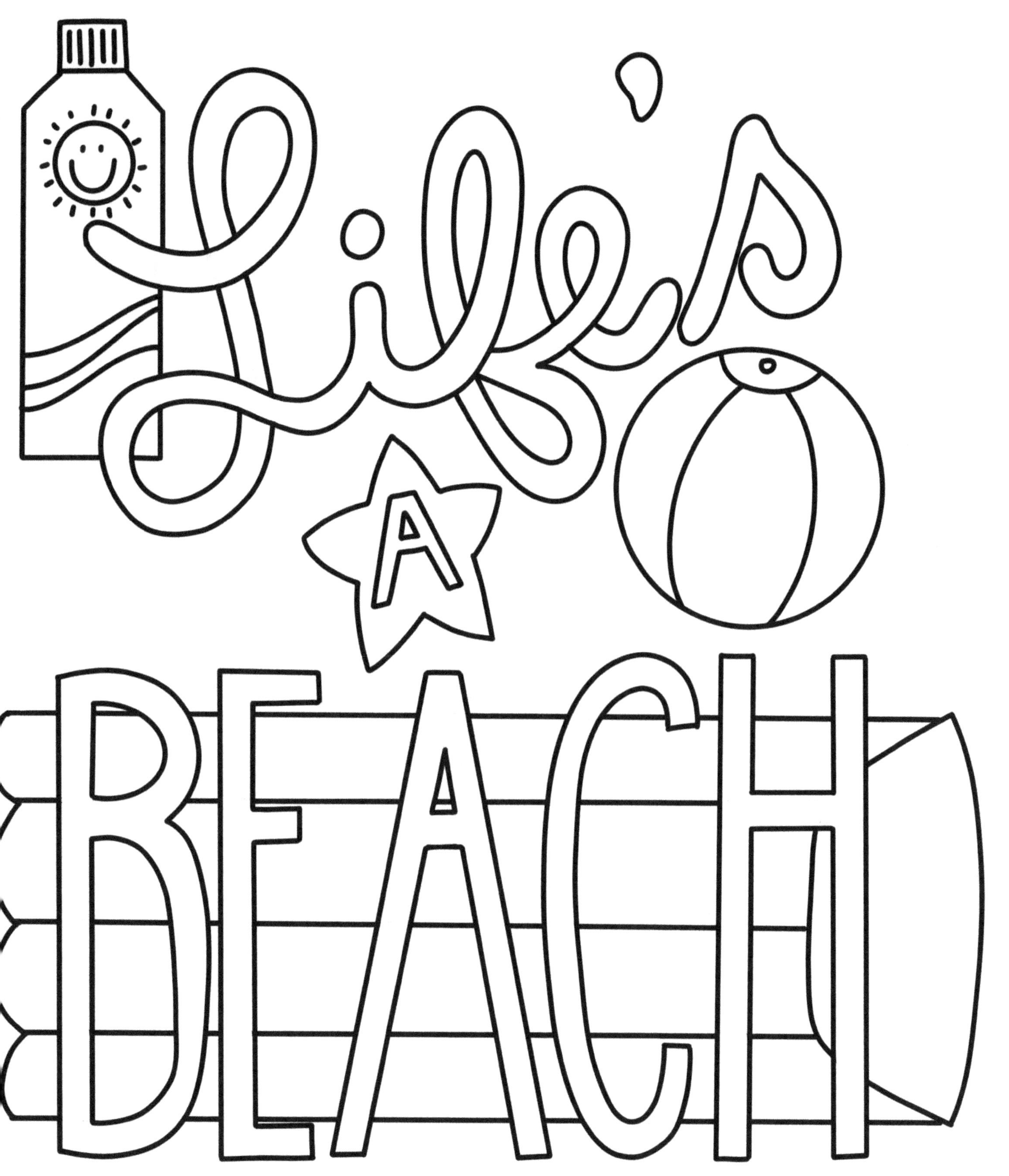
Life's
A
BEACH

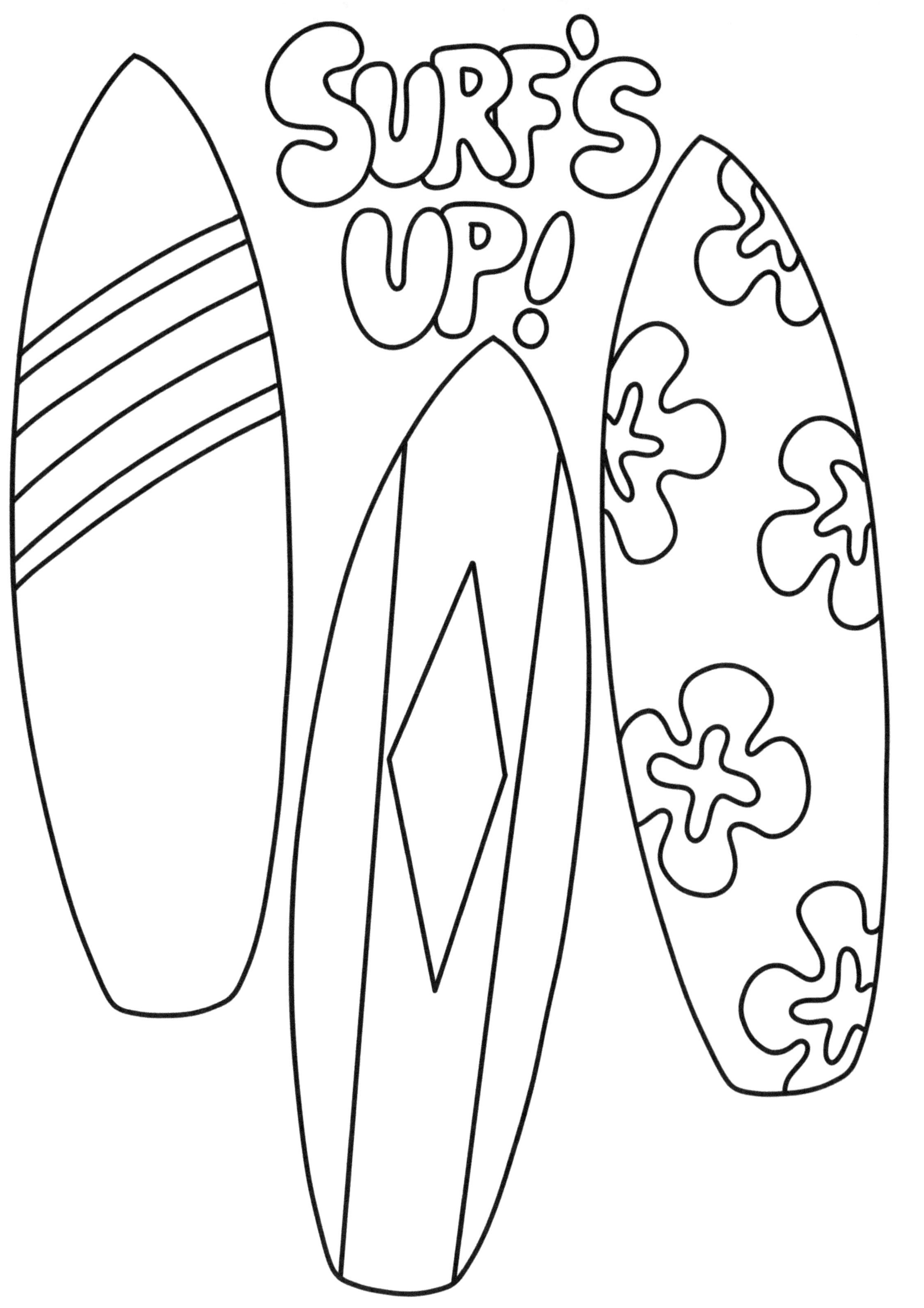
SURF'S UP!

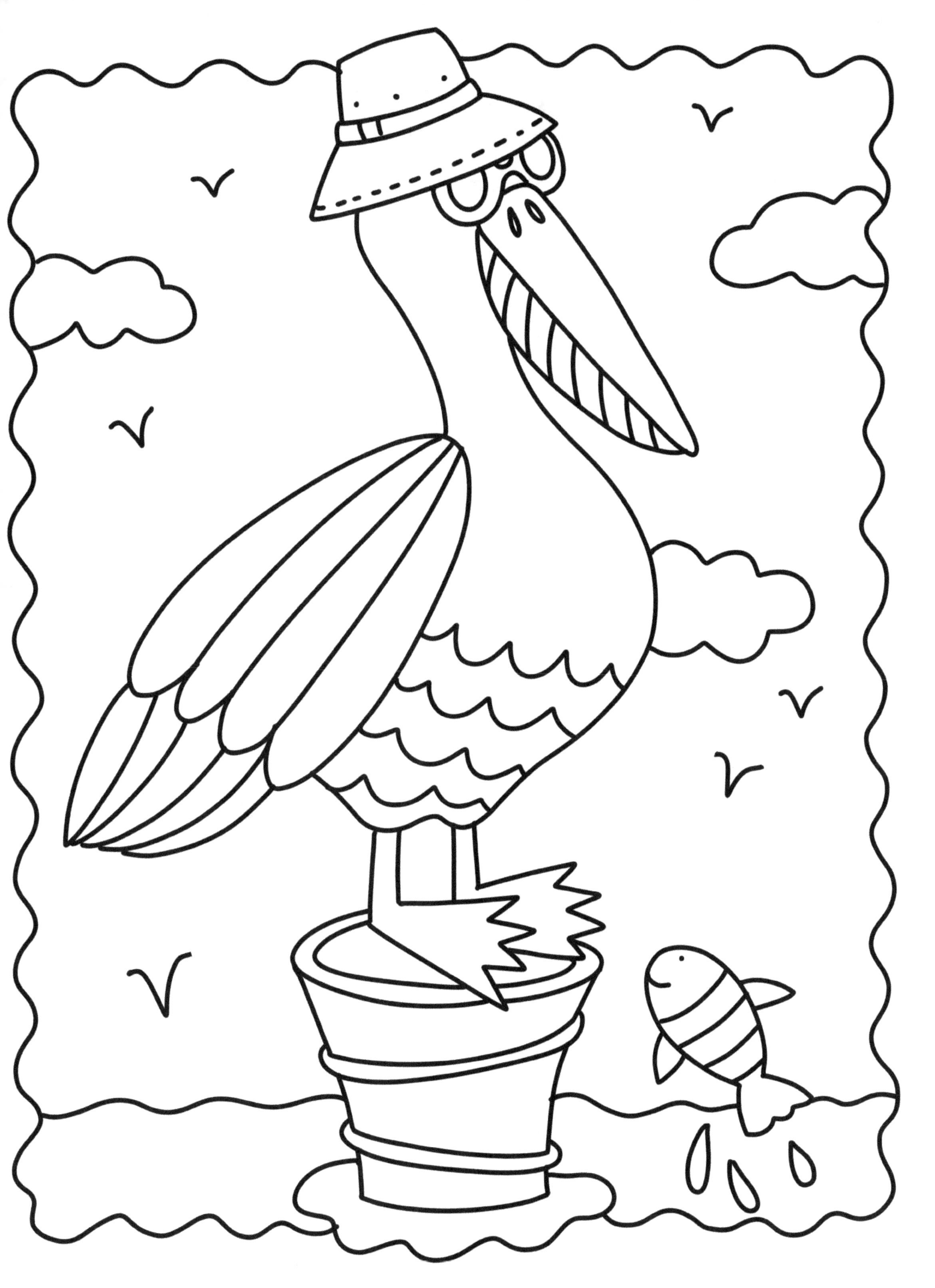

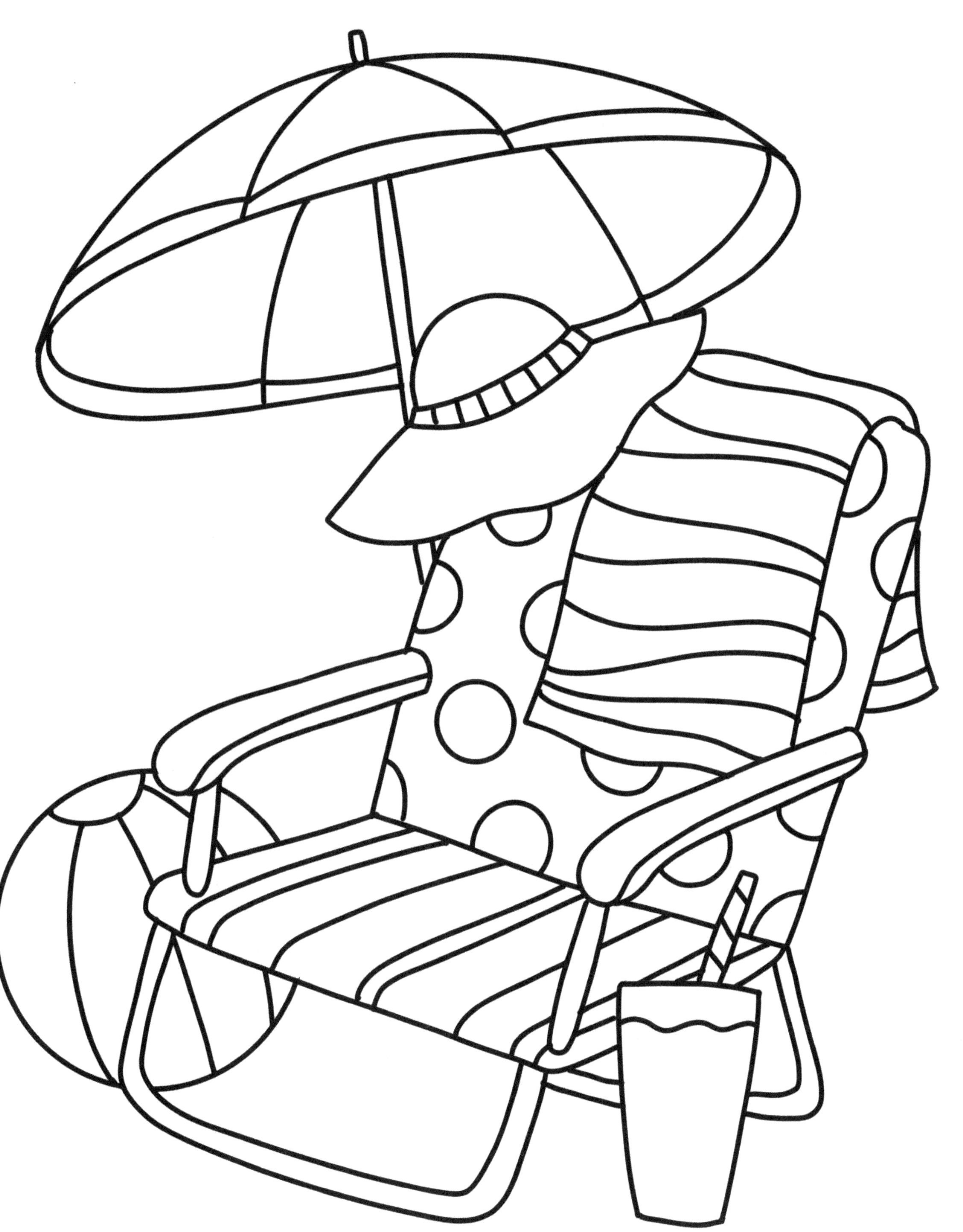

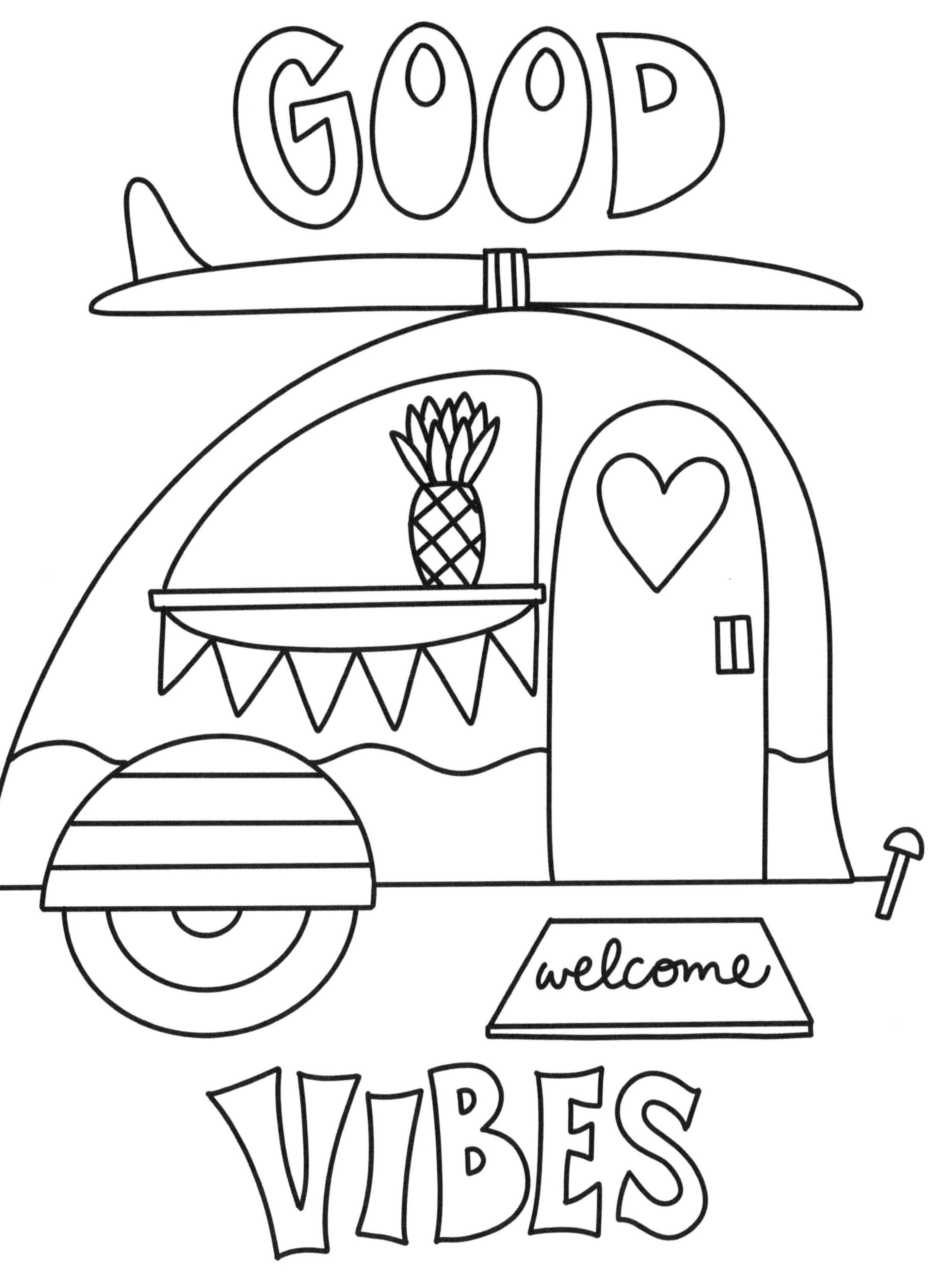
GOOD
welcome
VIBES

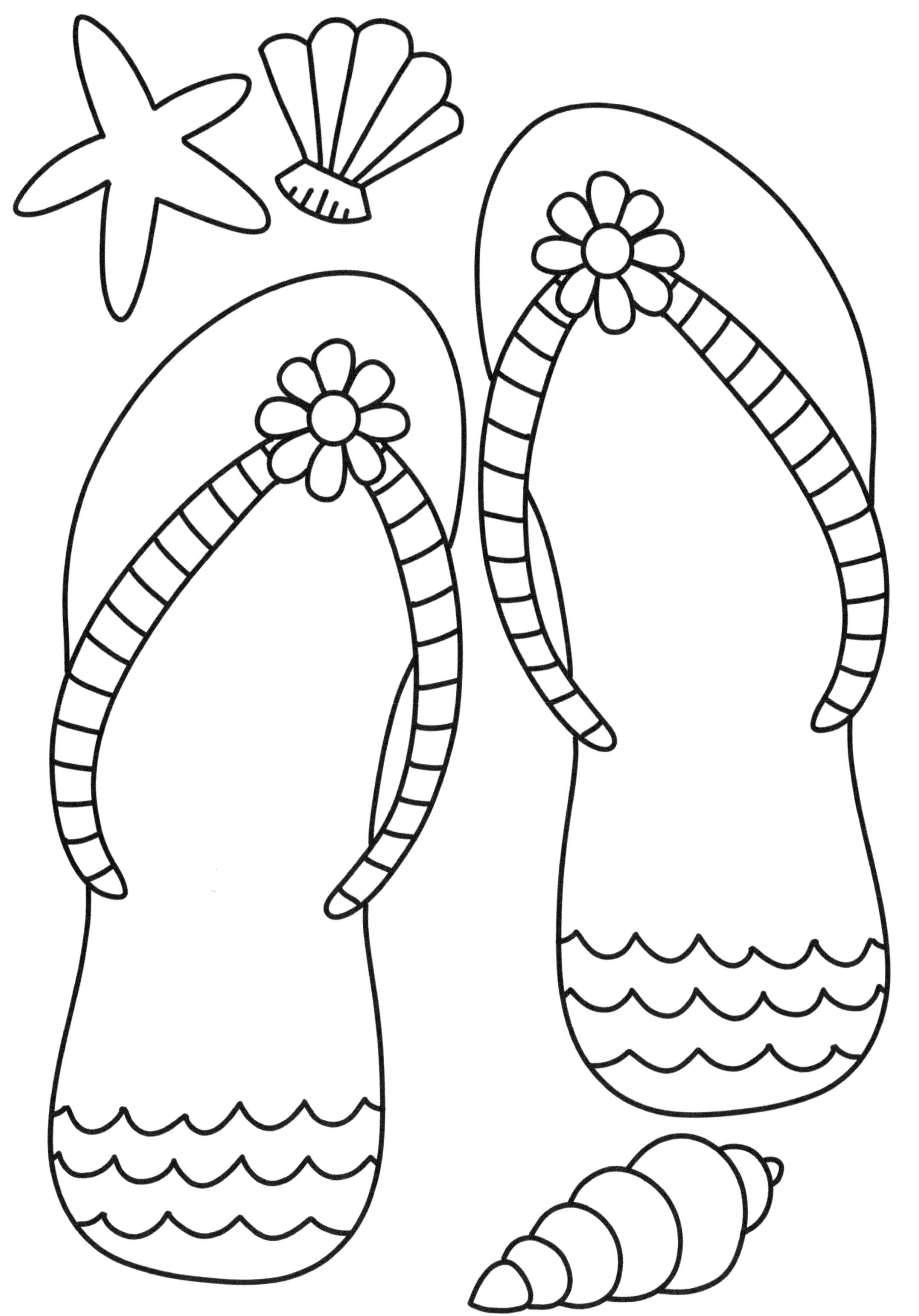

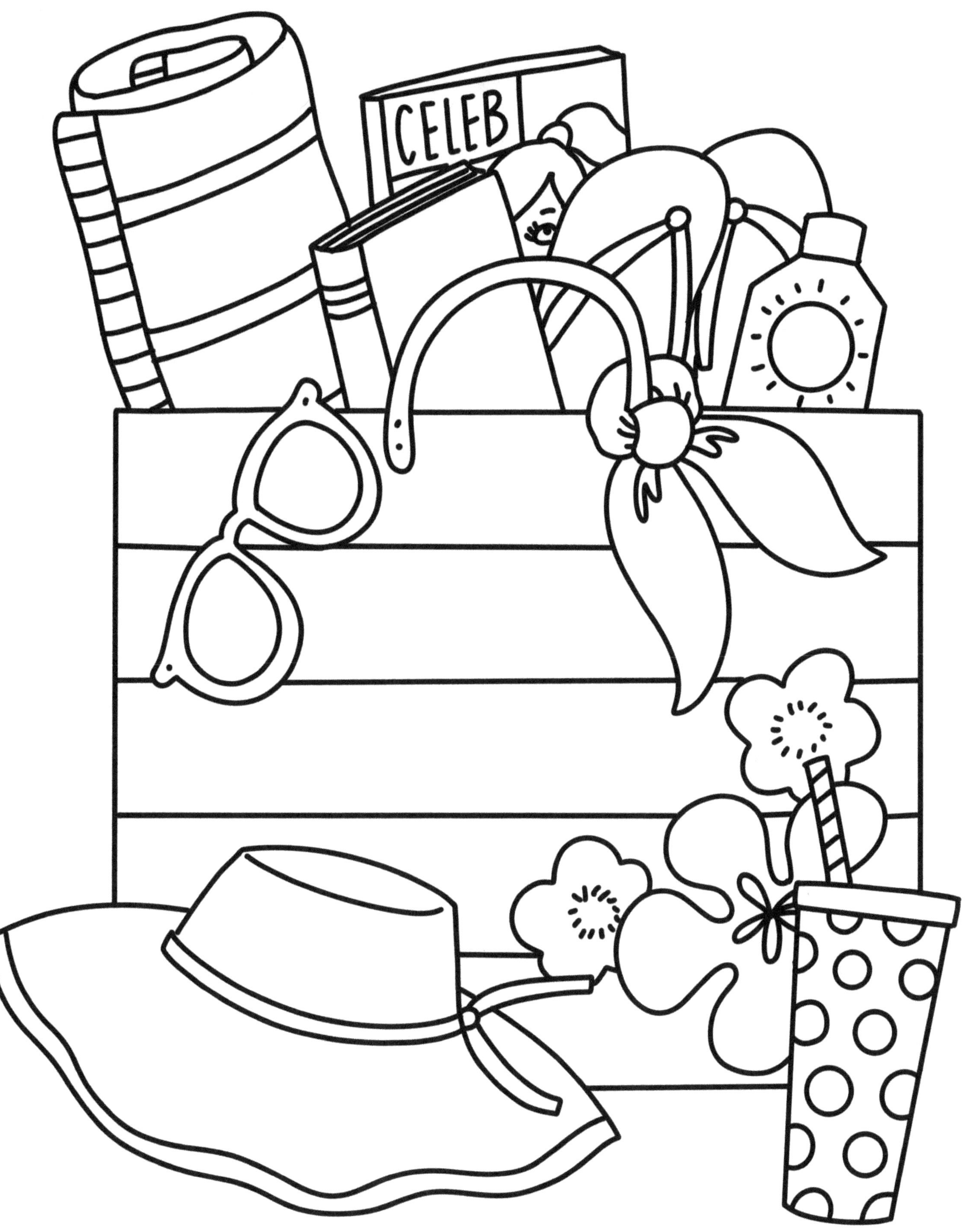
CELEB

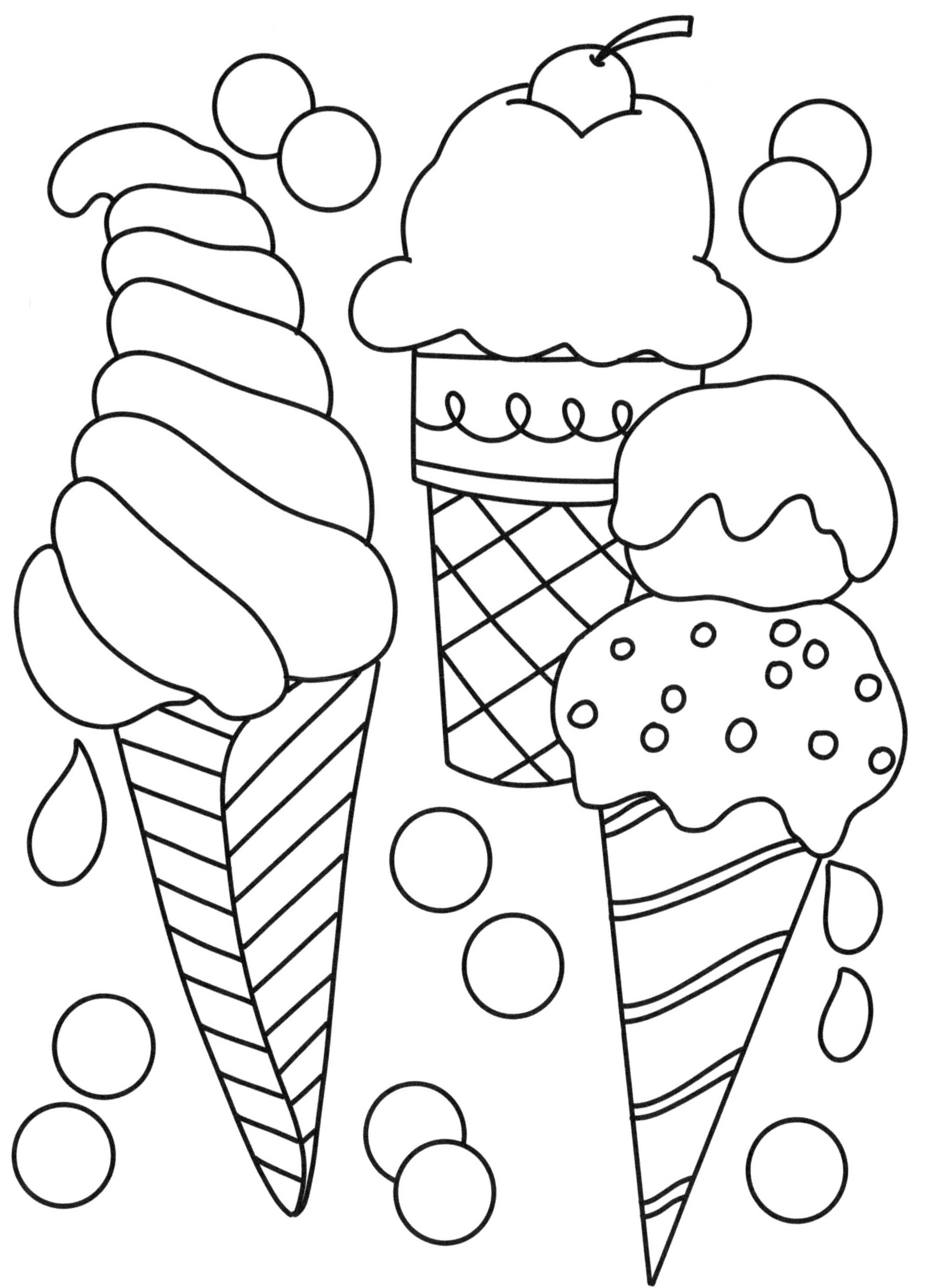

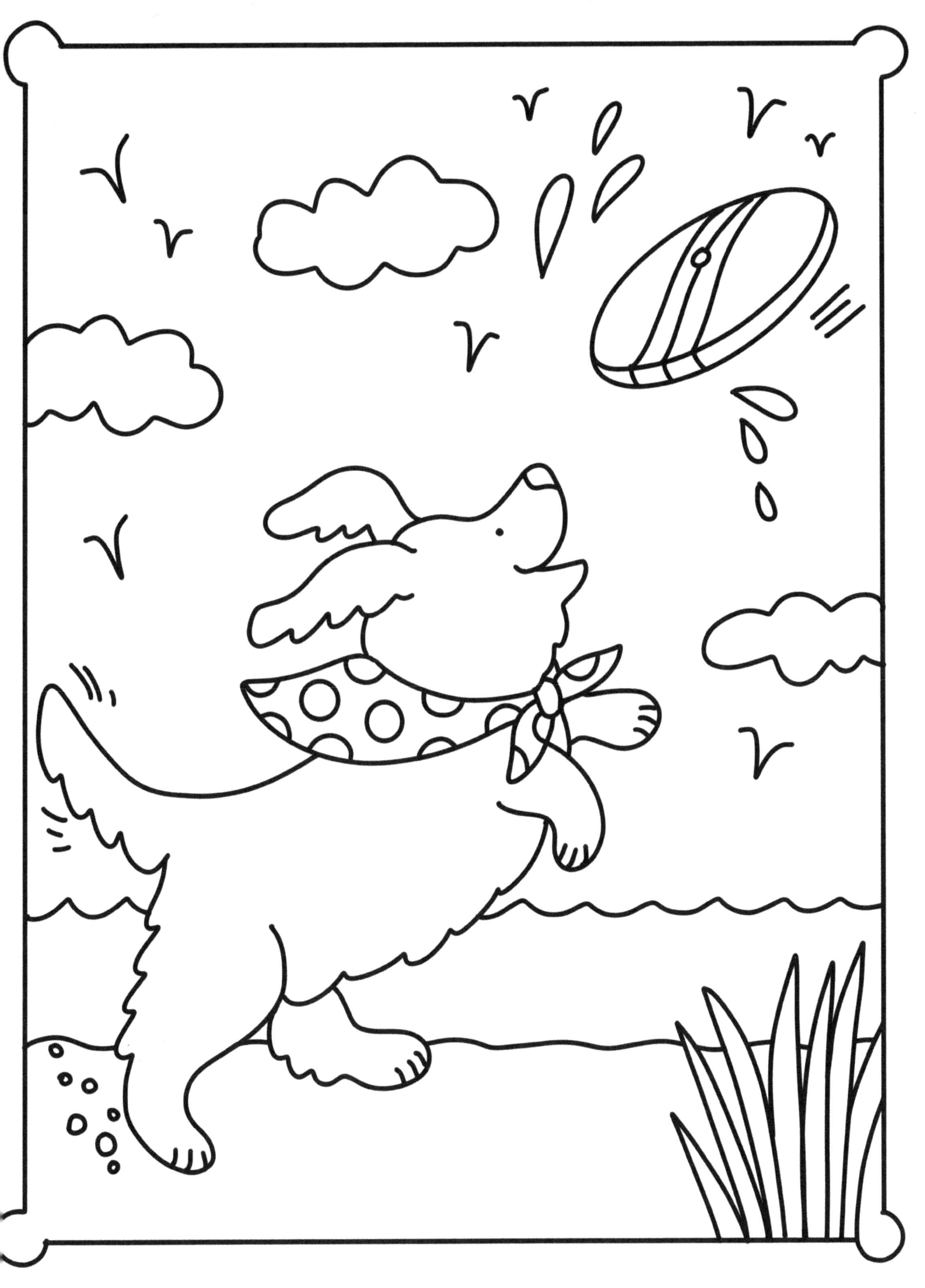

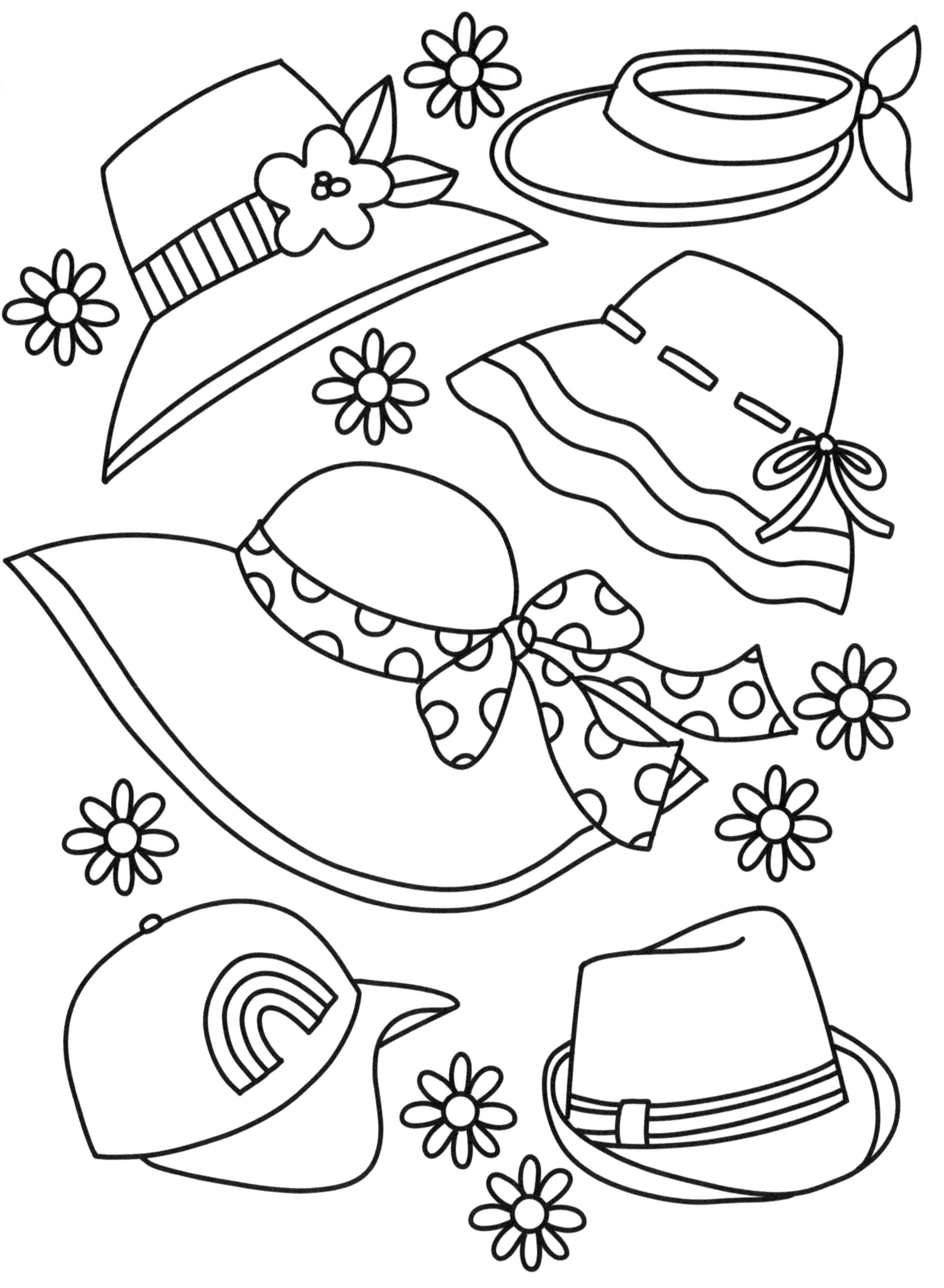

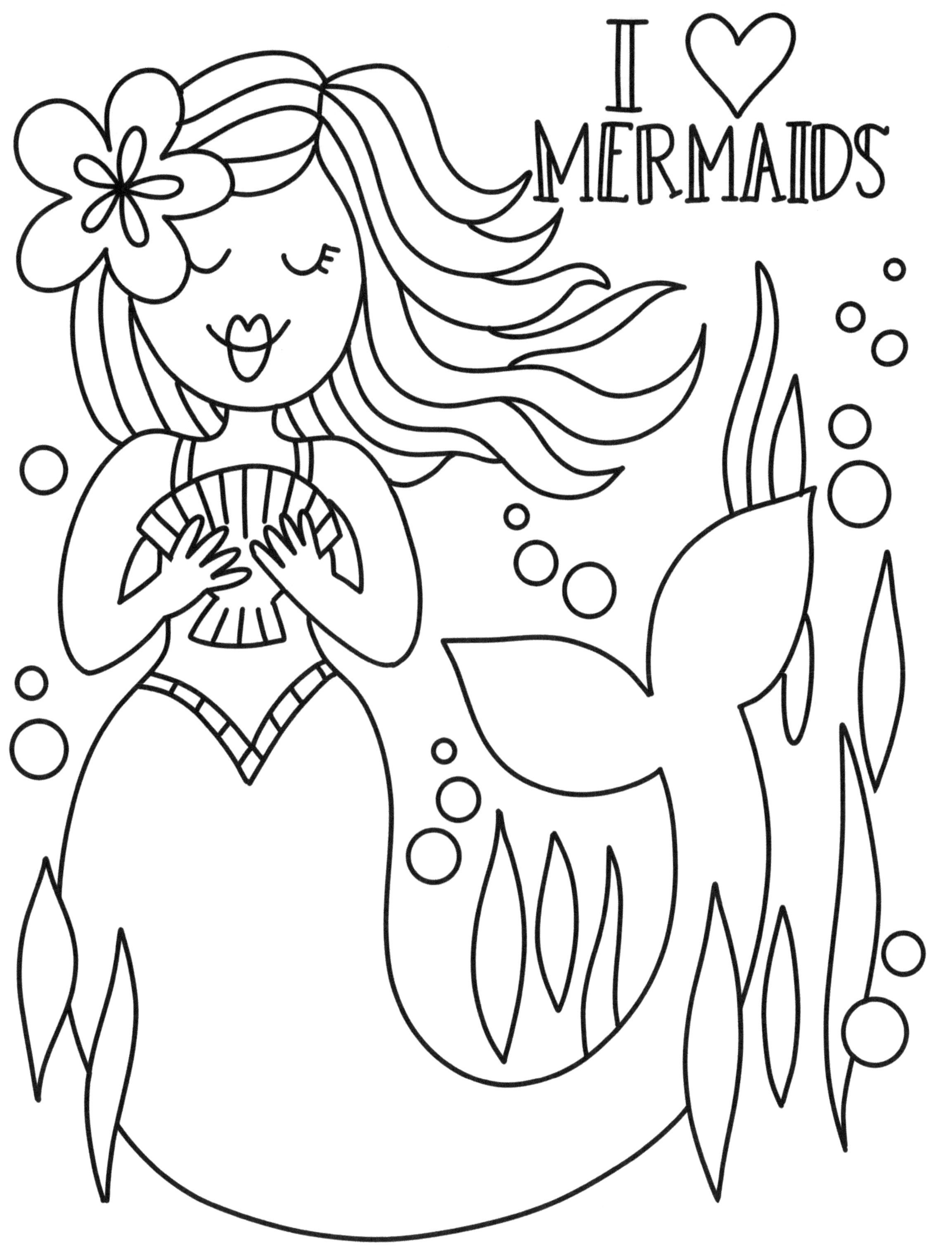
I ♡
MERMAIDS

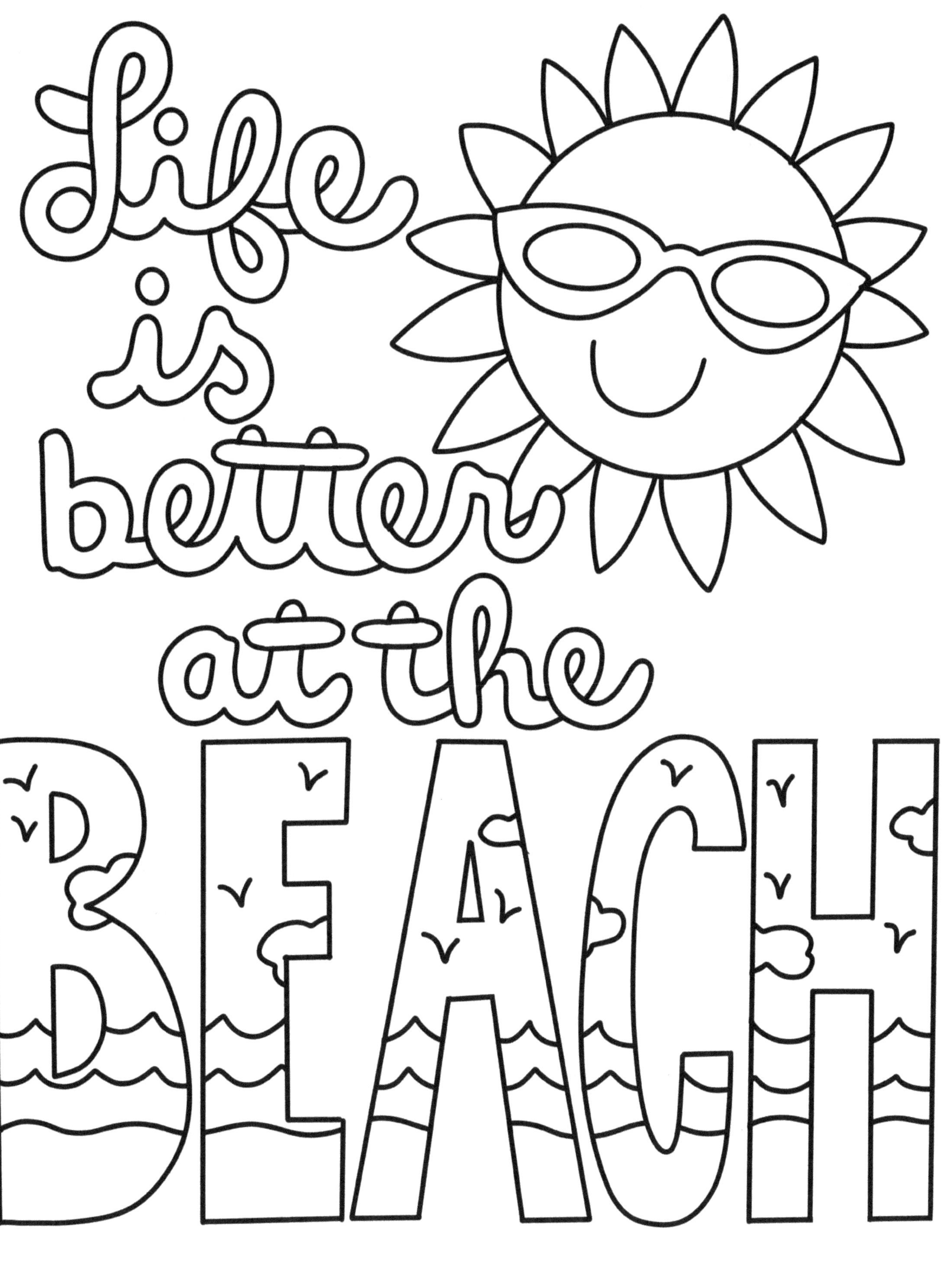
life
is
better
at the
BEACH

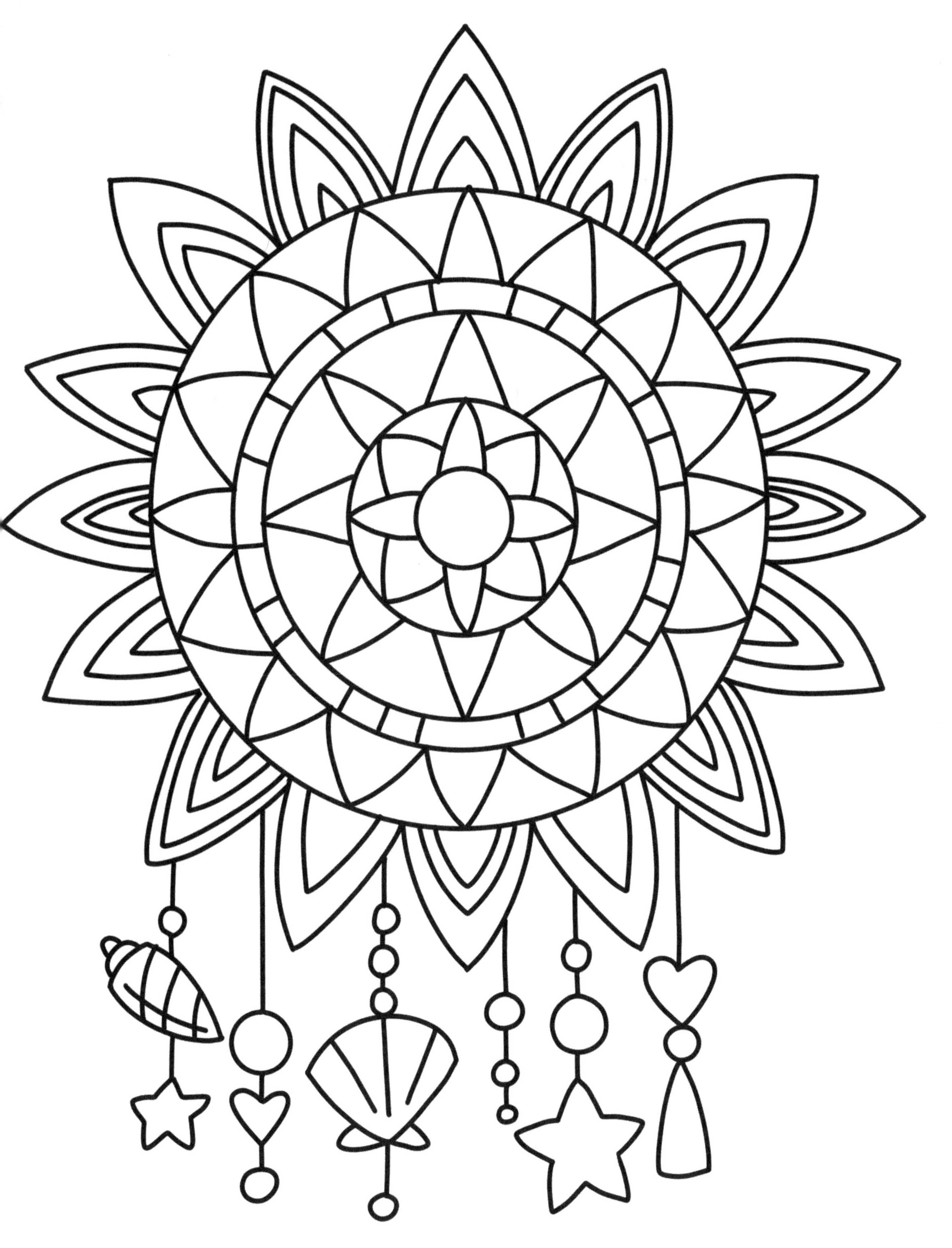

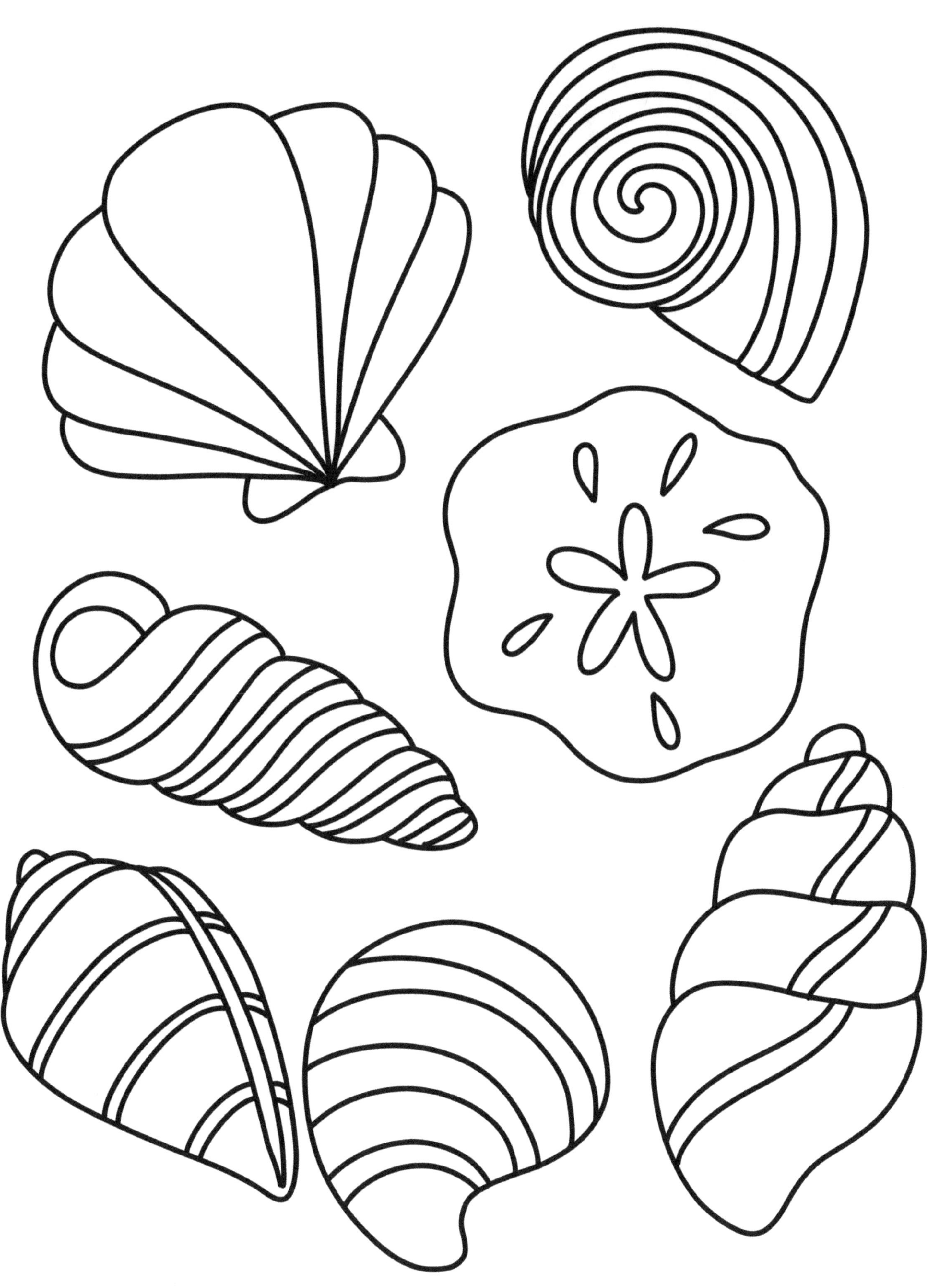

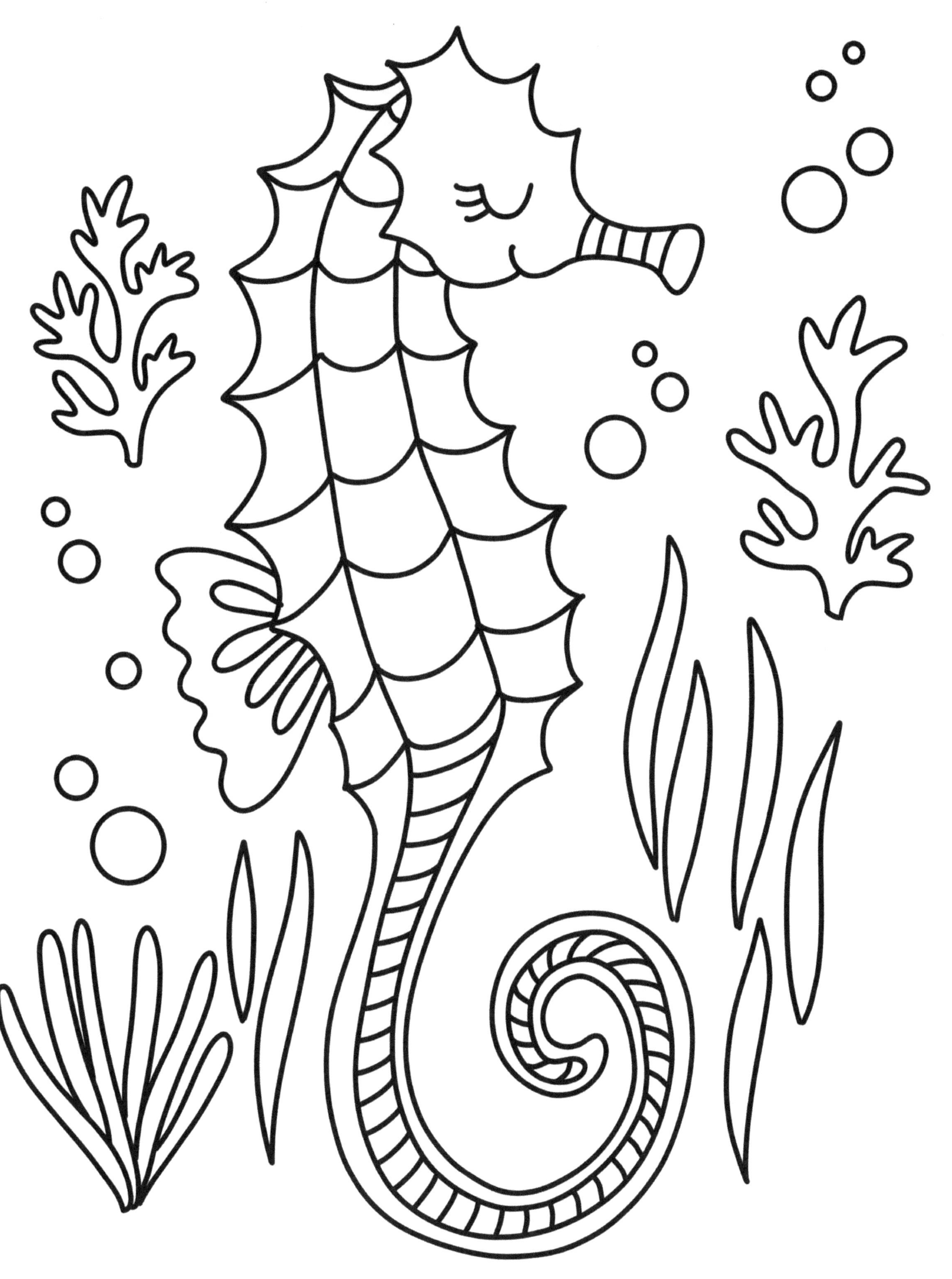

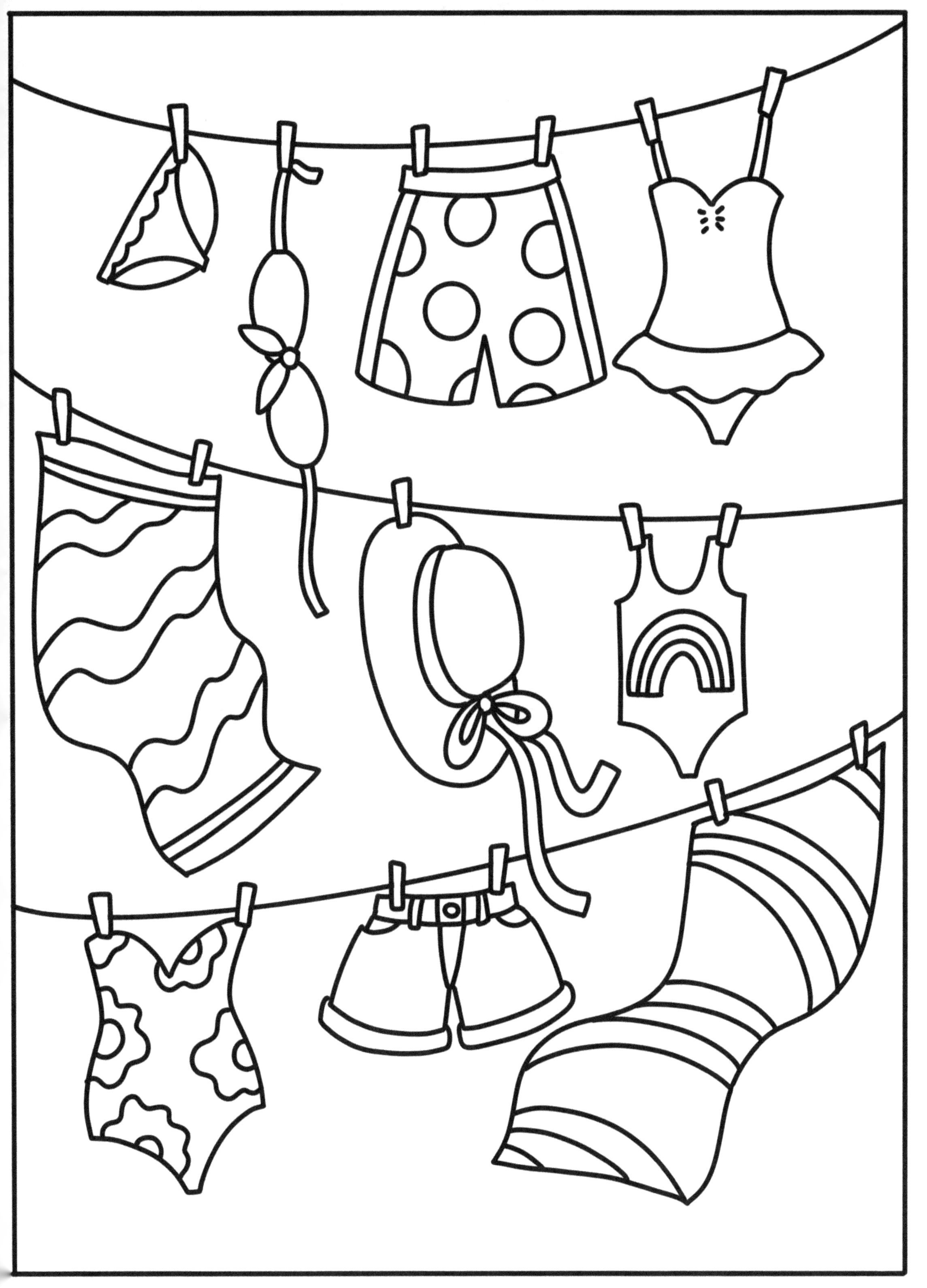

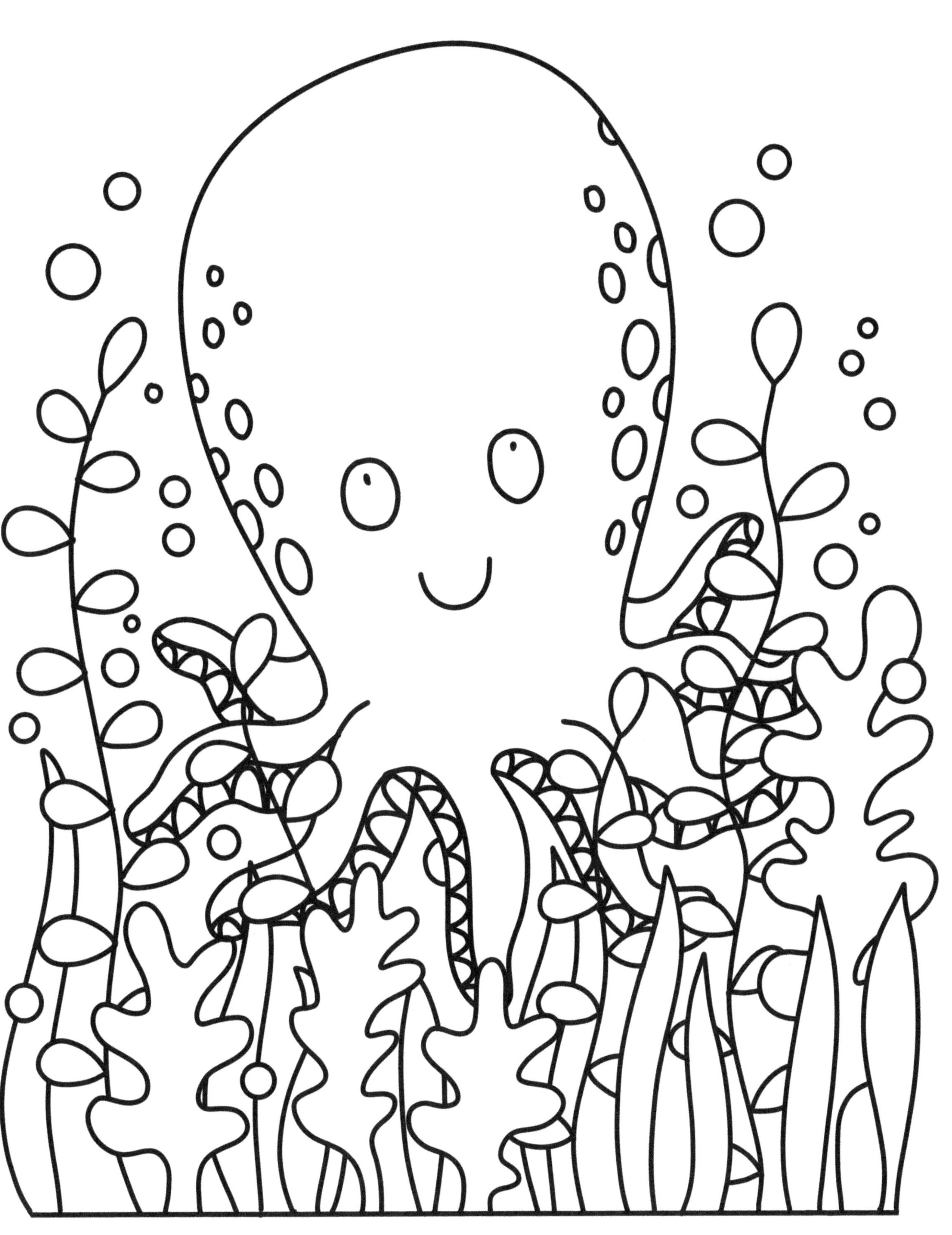

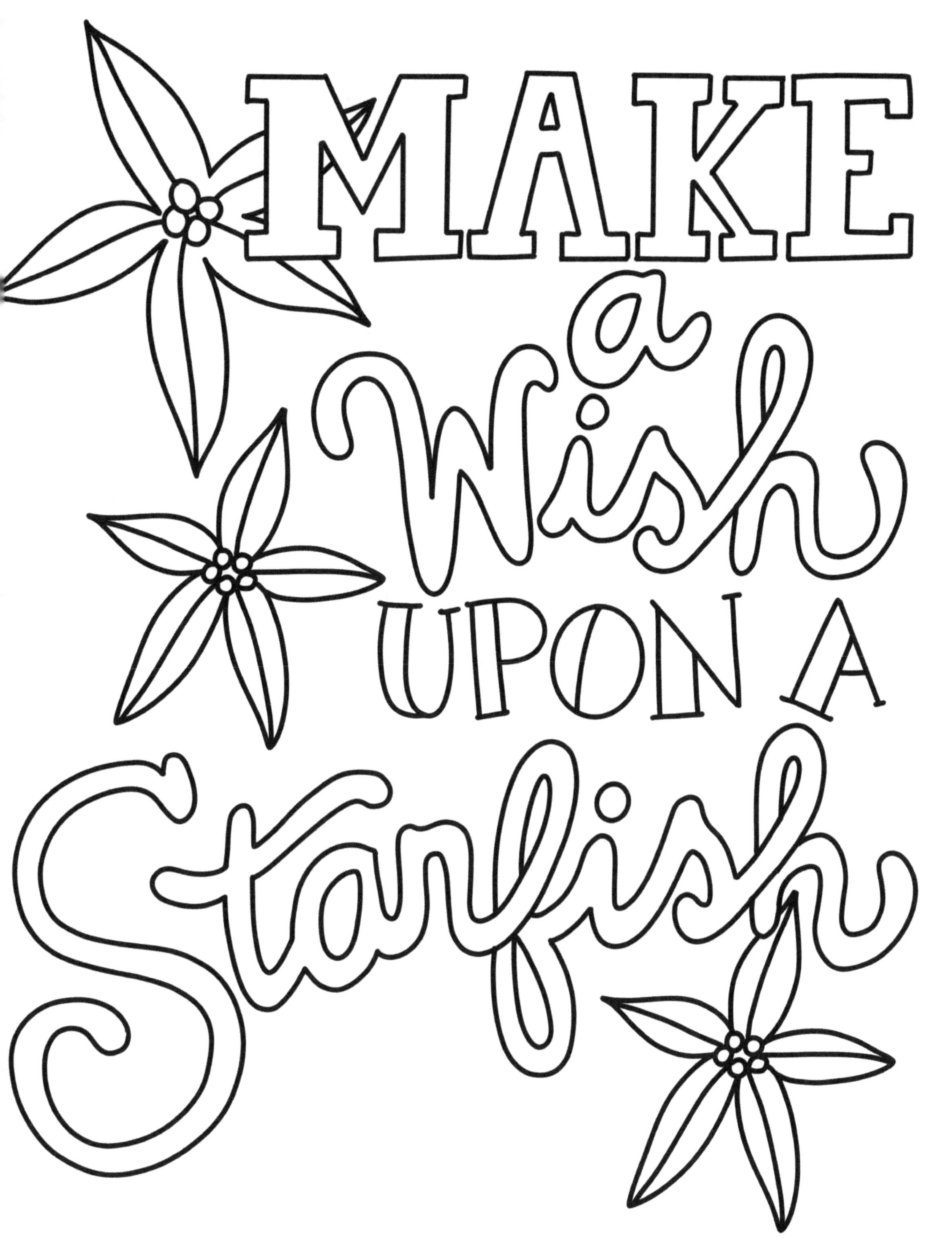
MAKE
a
Wish
UPON A
Starfish

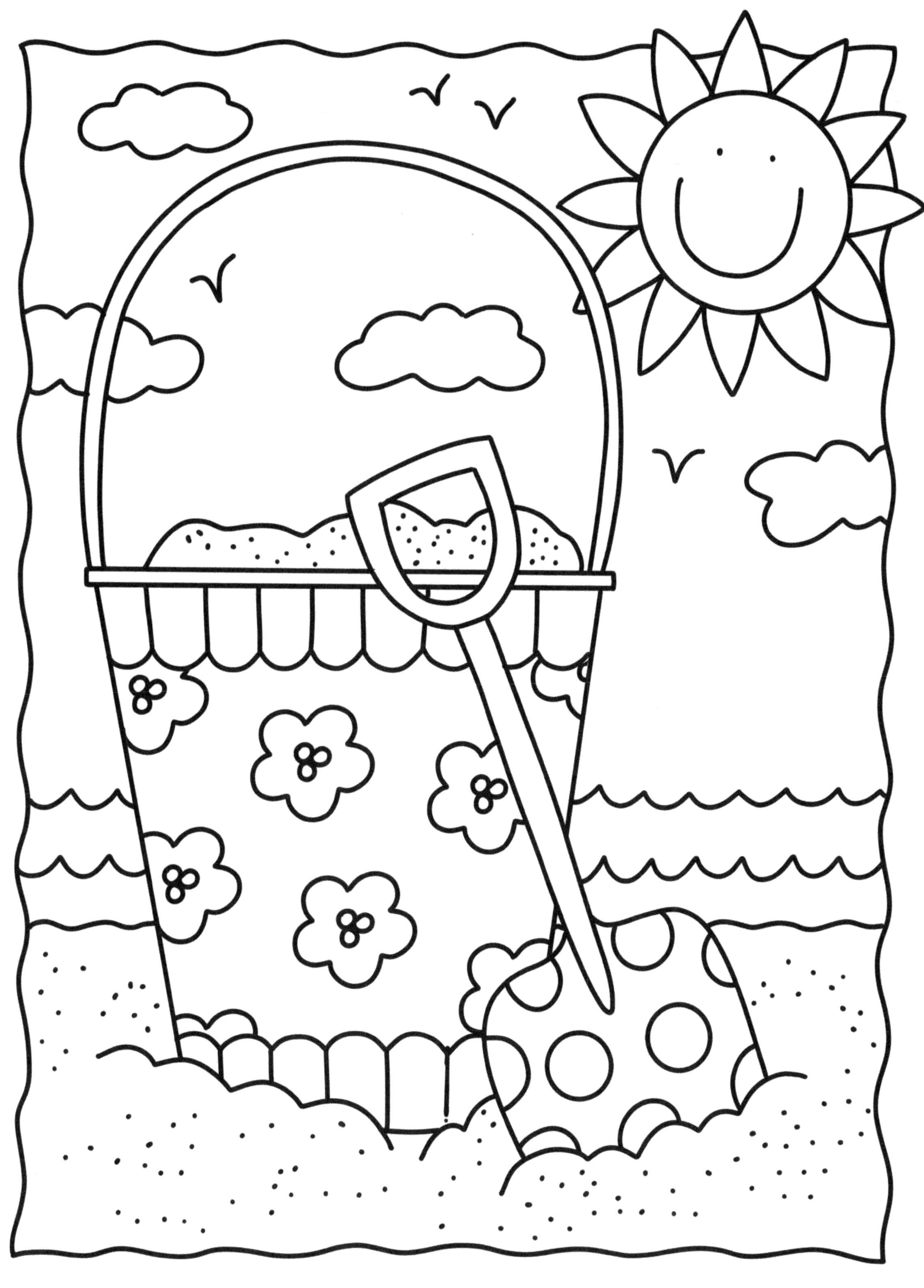

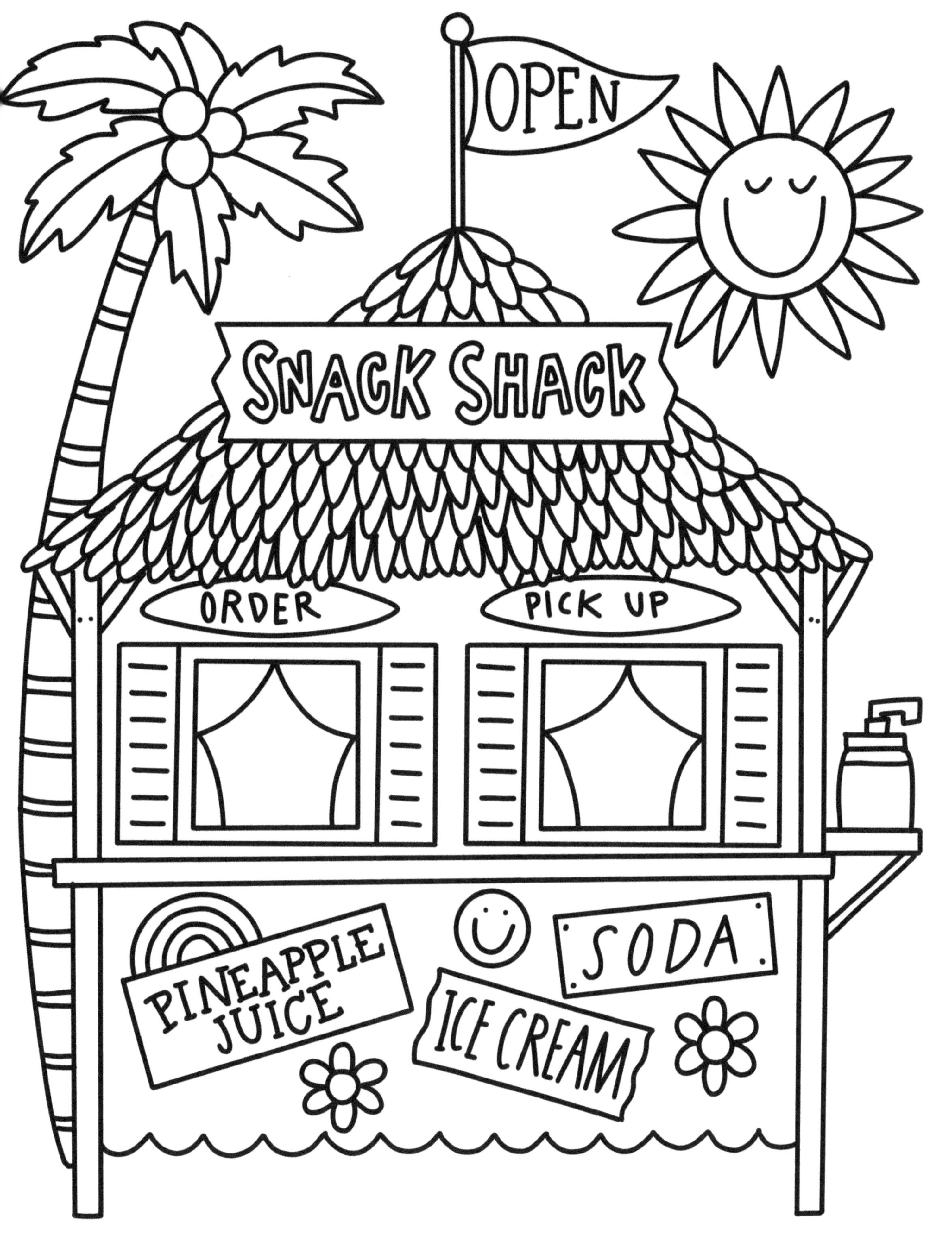
OPEN
SNACK SHACK
ORDER
PICK UP
PINEAPPLE JUICE
SODA
ICE CREAM

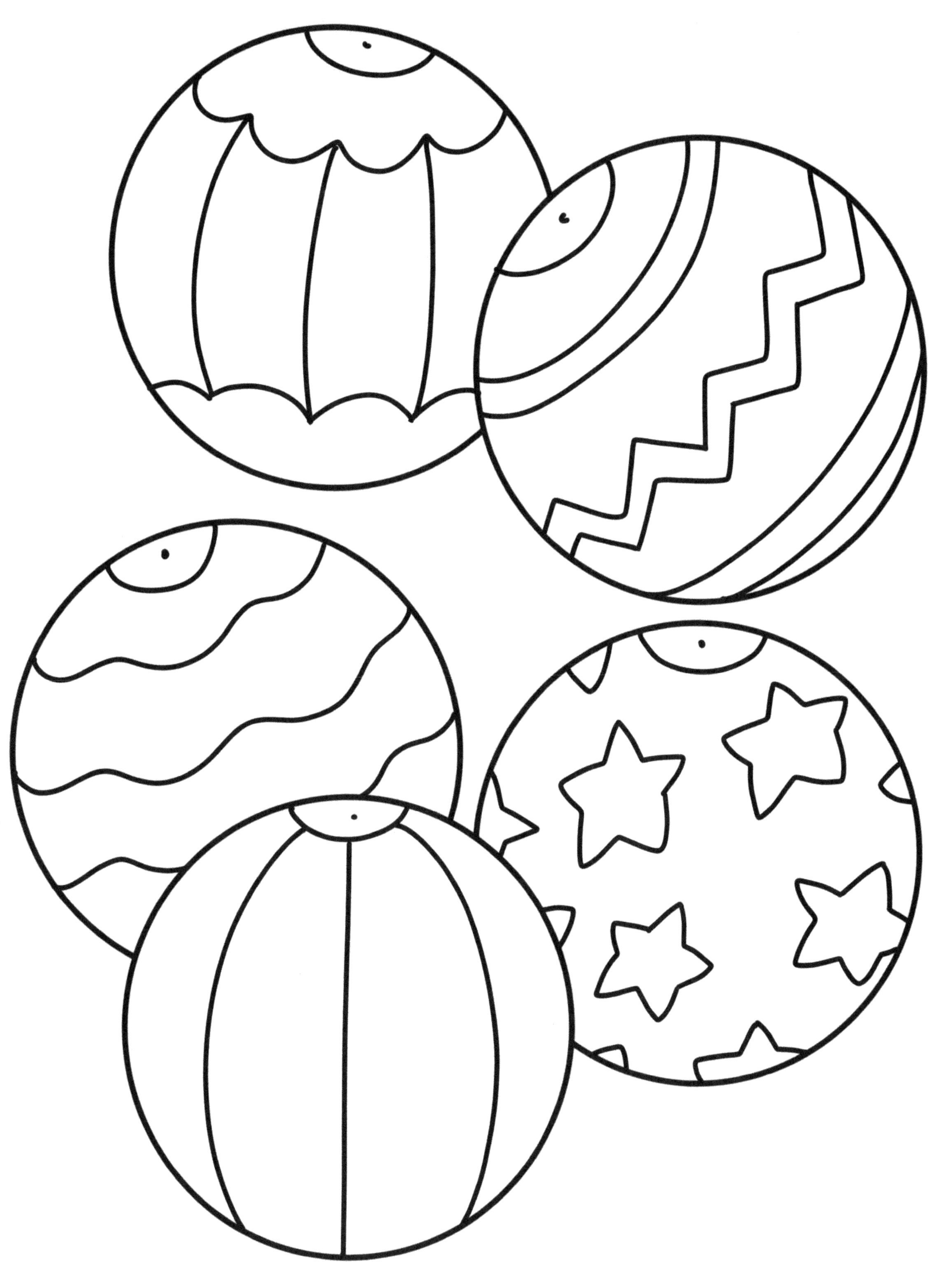

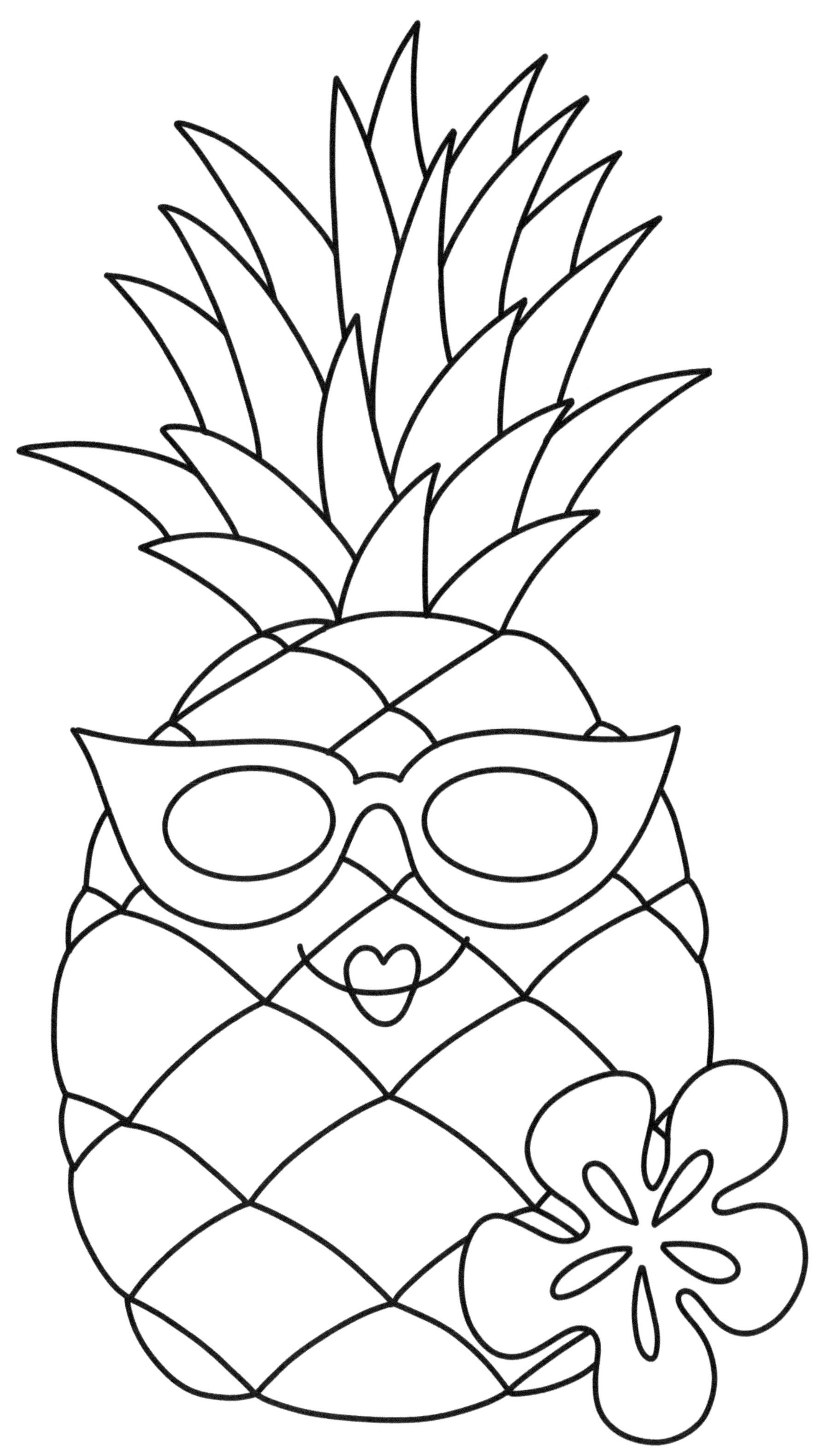

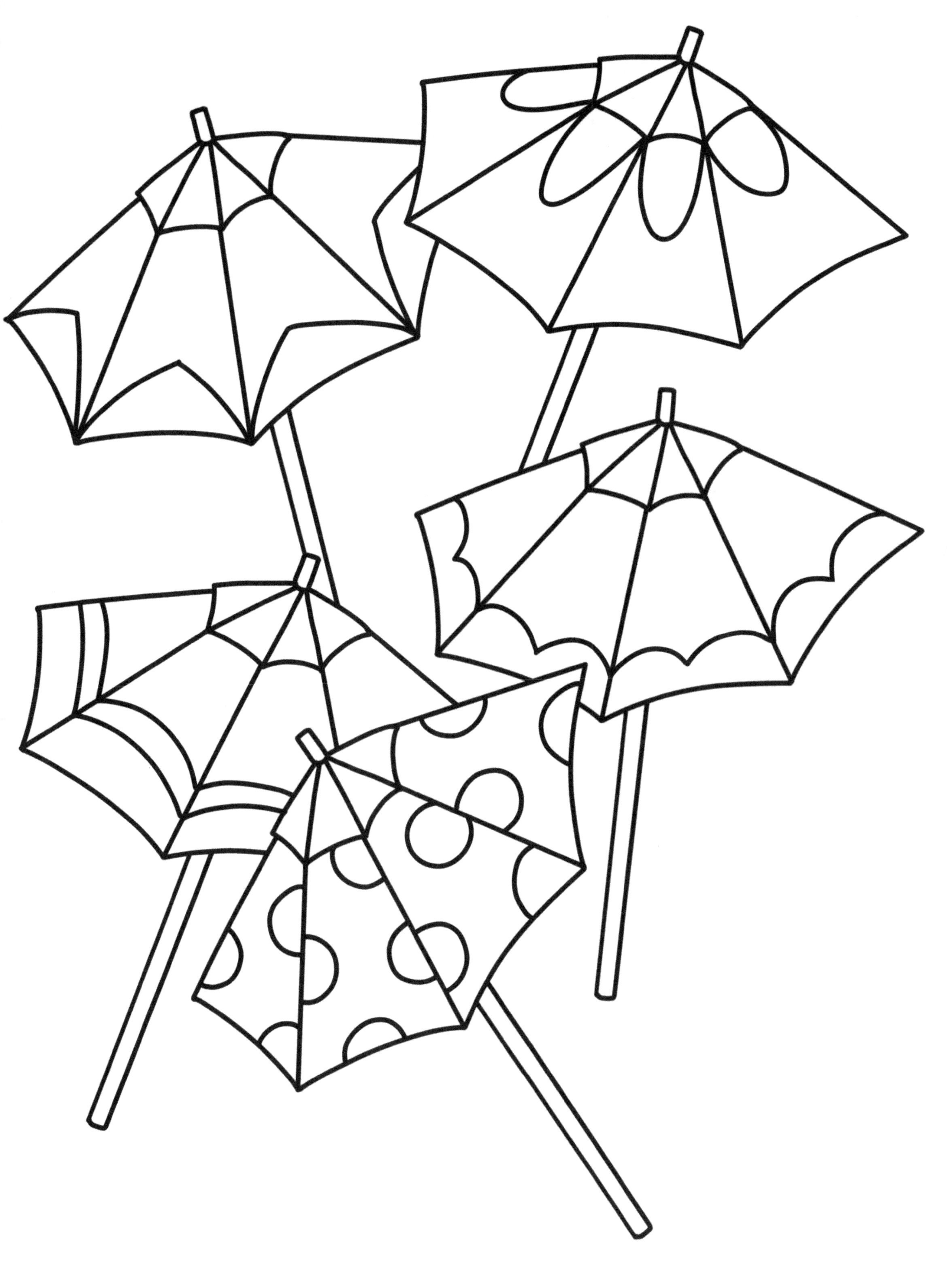

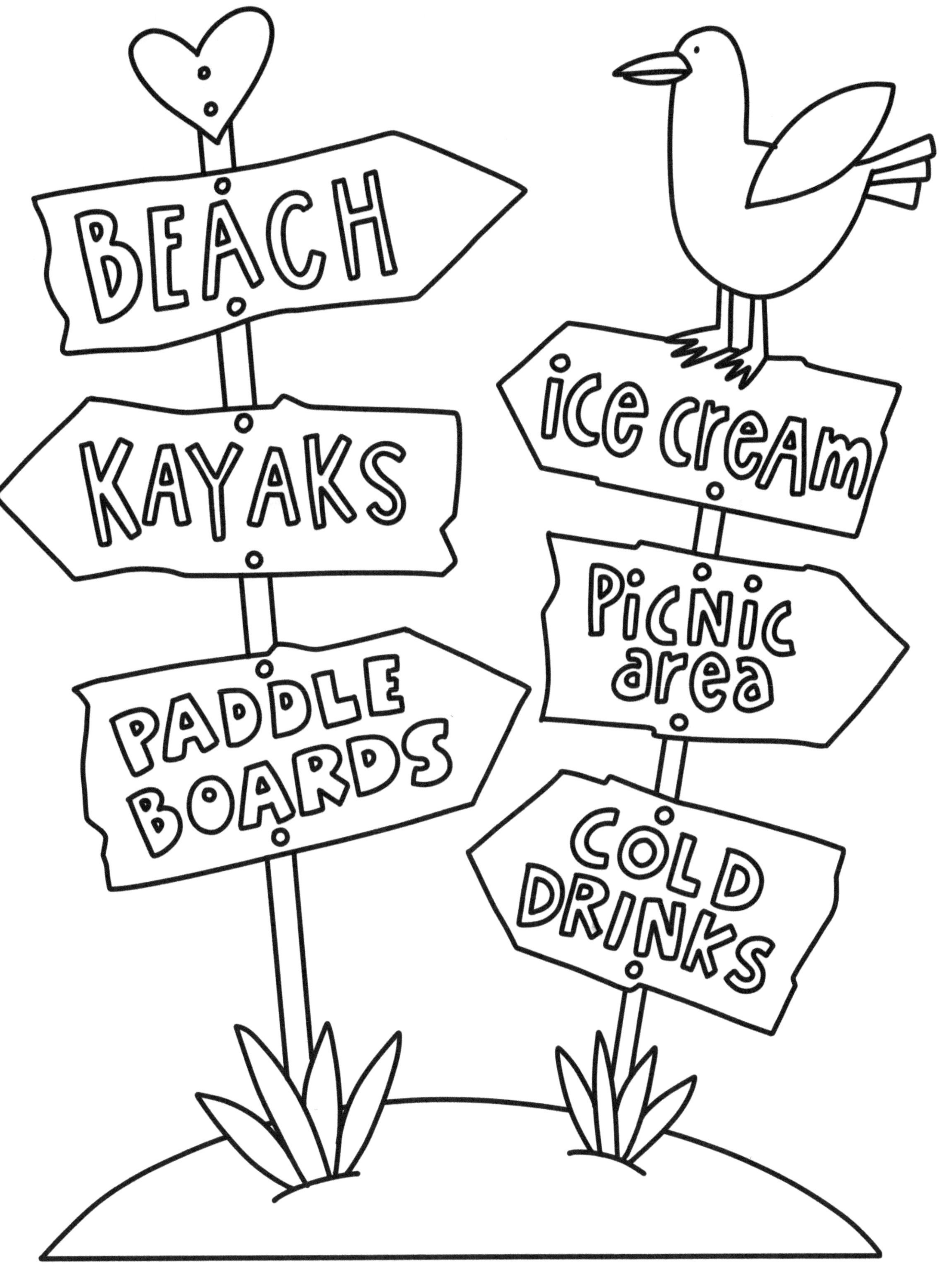
BEACH
KAYAKS
PADDLE BOARDS
ice cream
Picnic area
COLD DRINKS

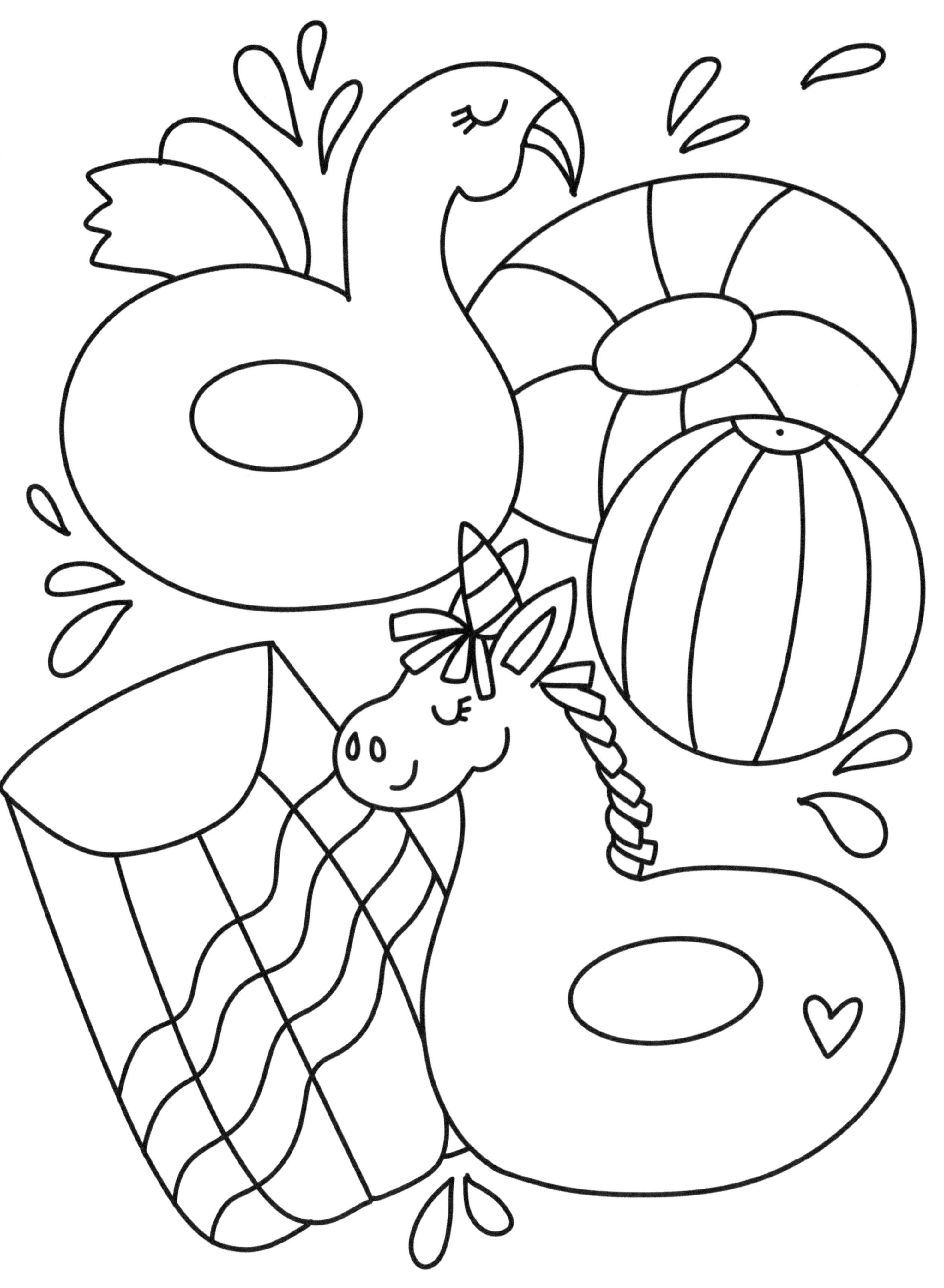

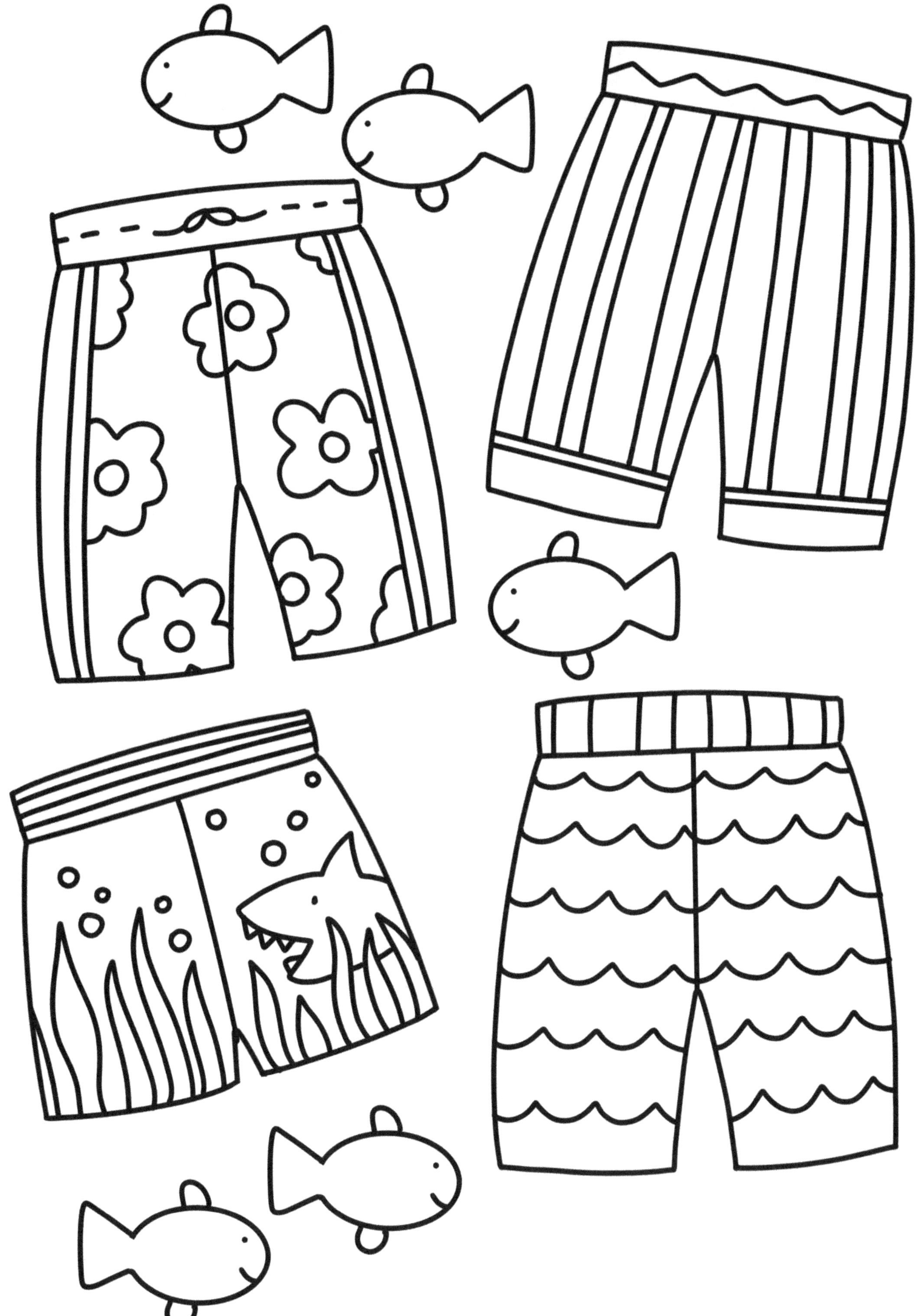

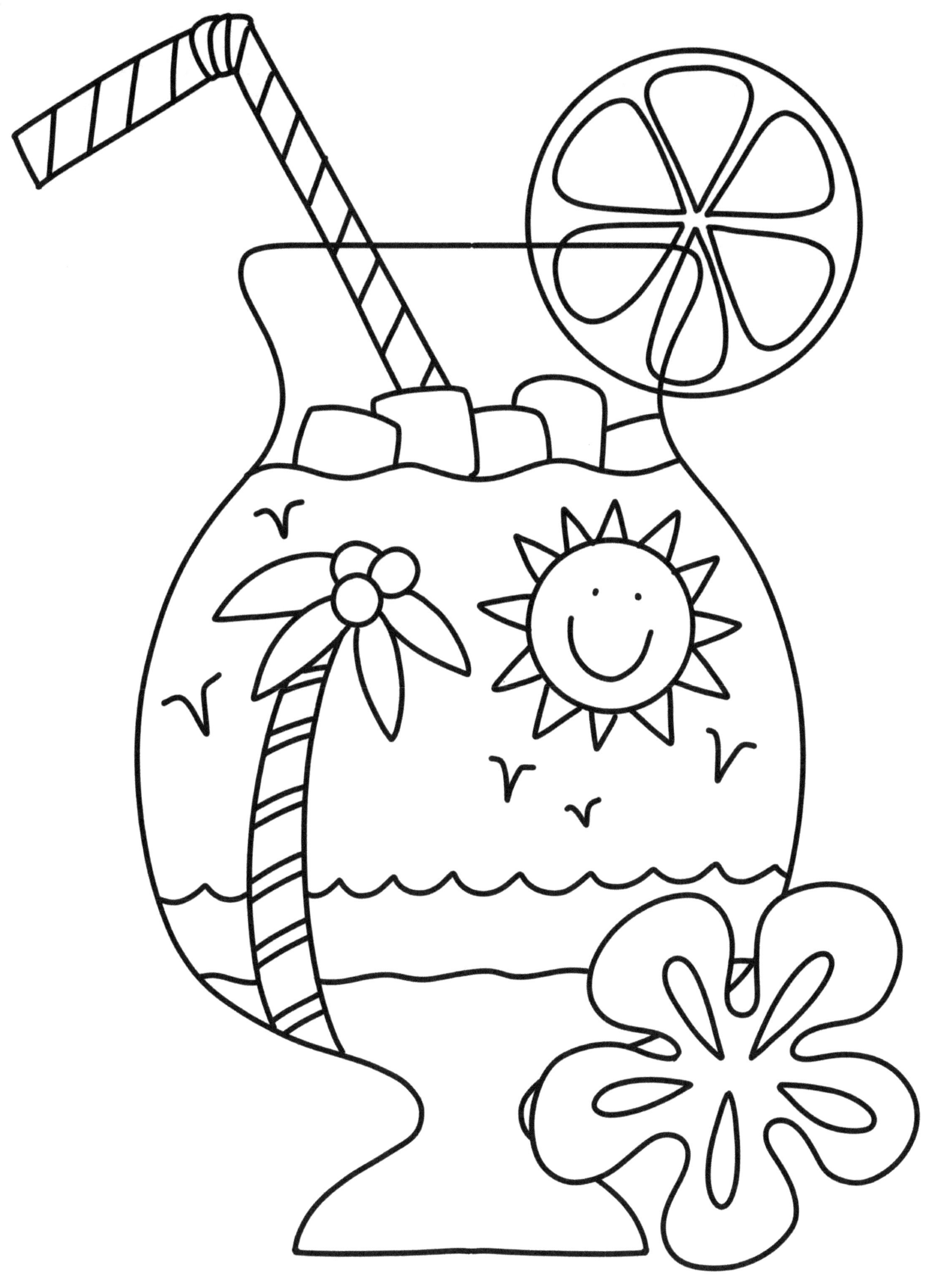

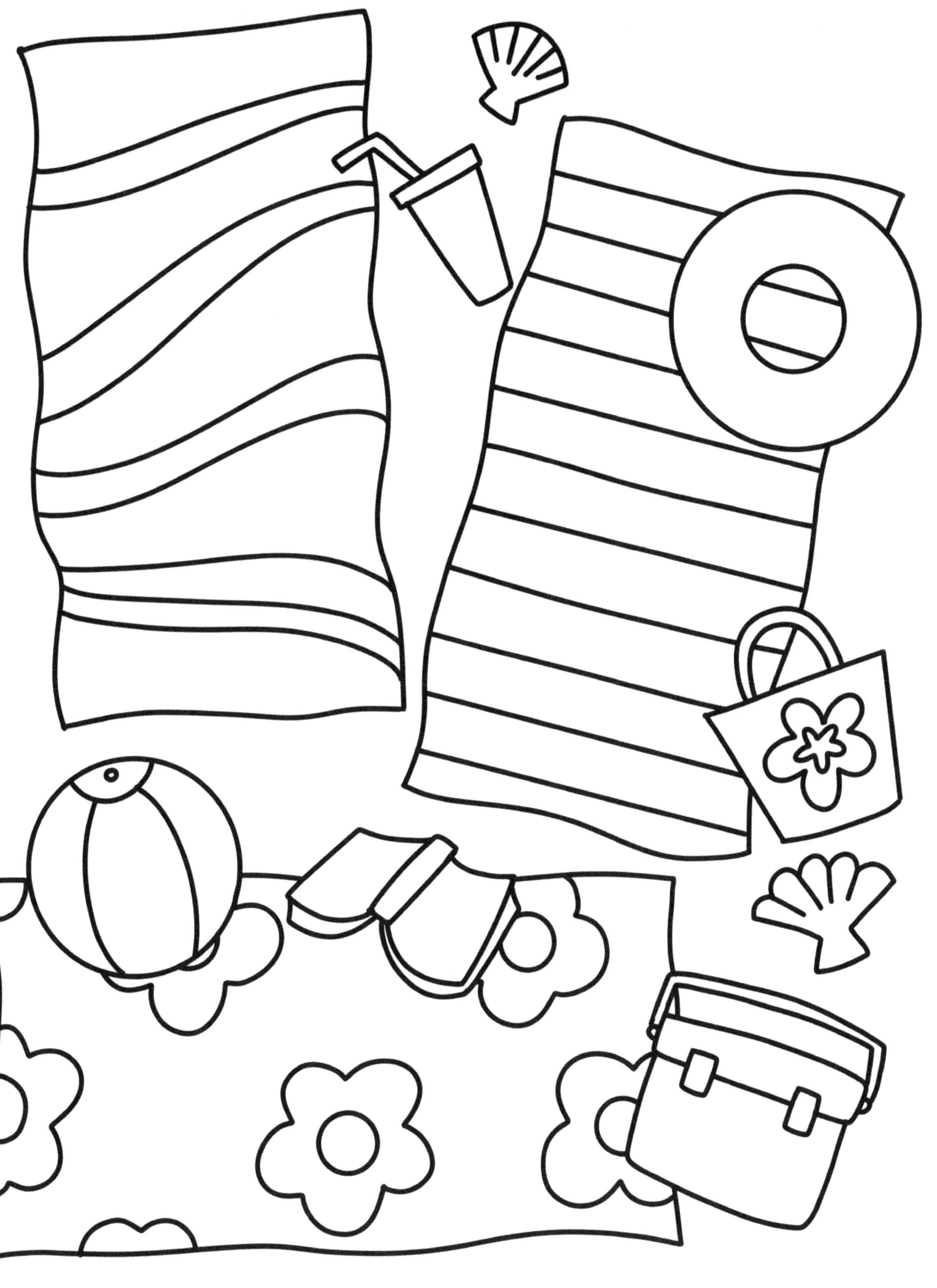

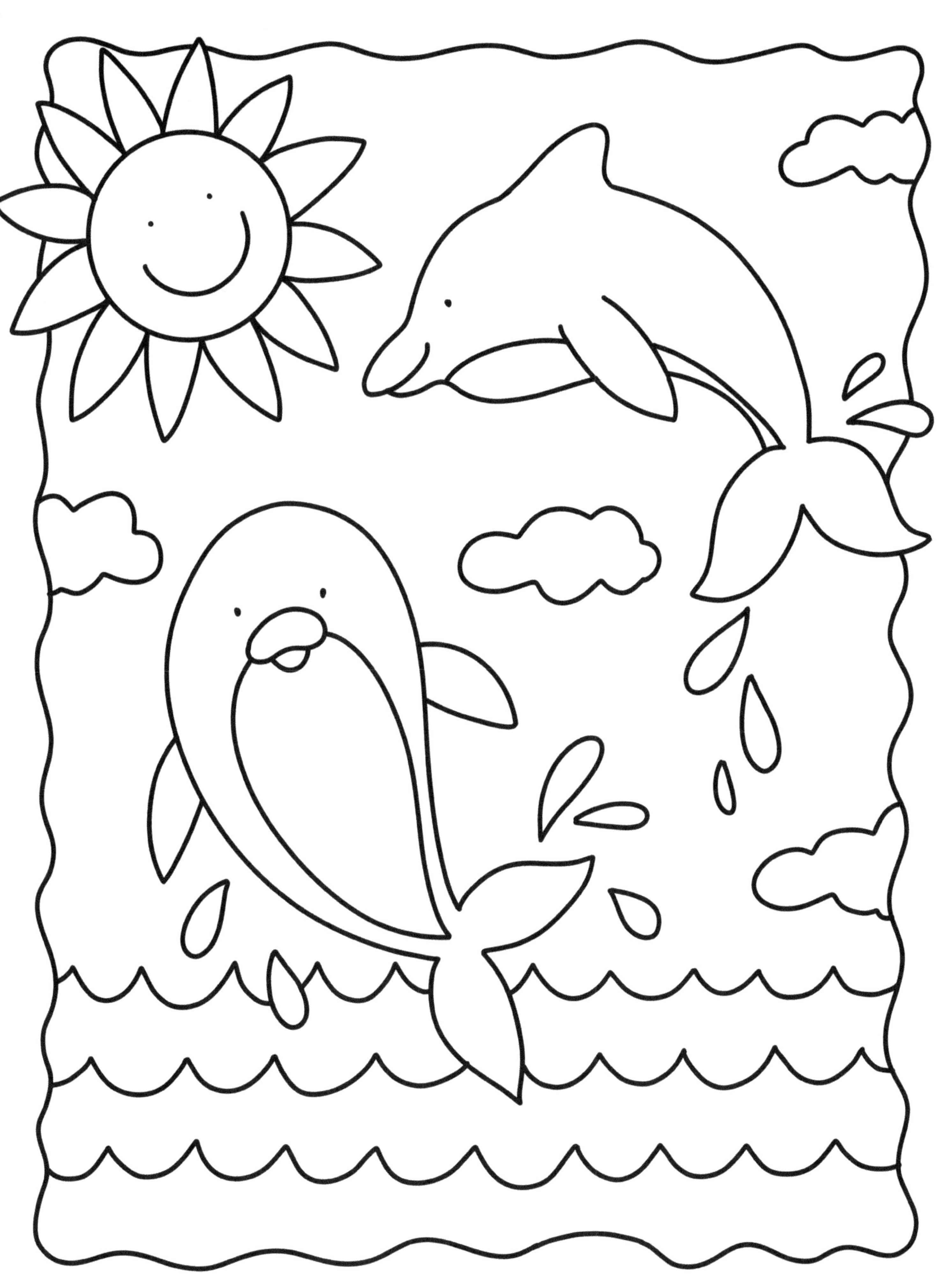

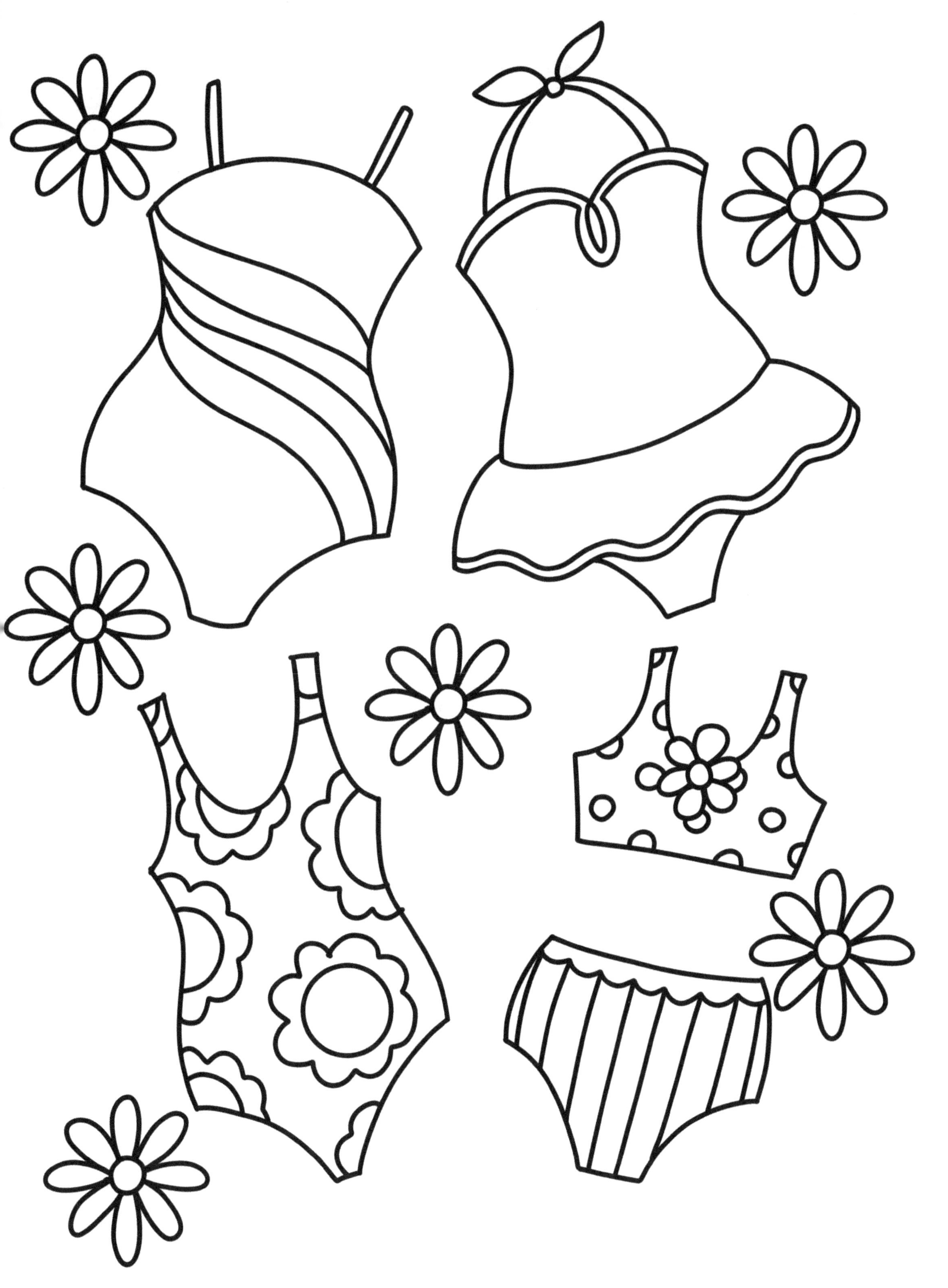

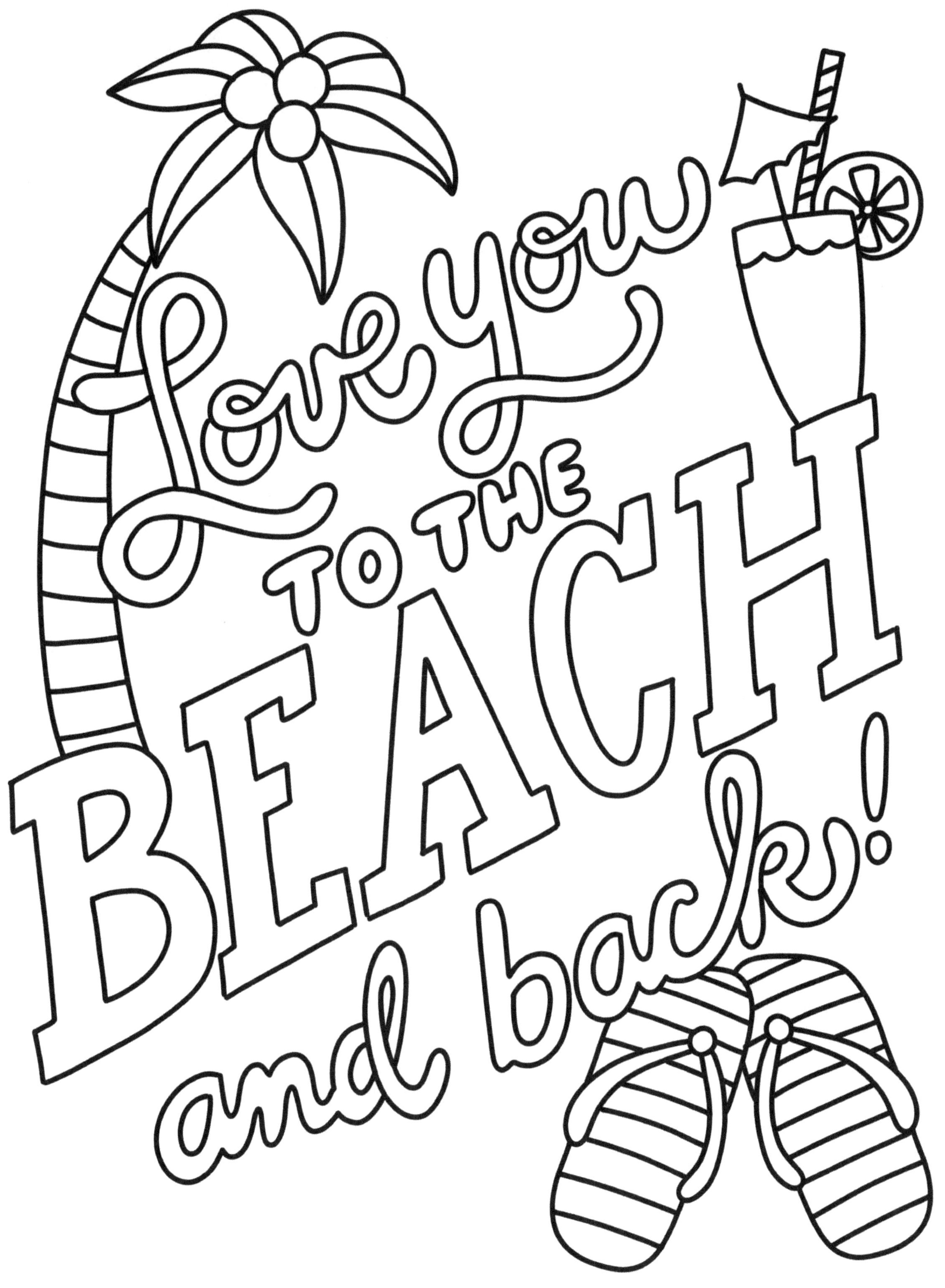
Love you
TO THE
BEACH
and back!

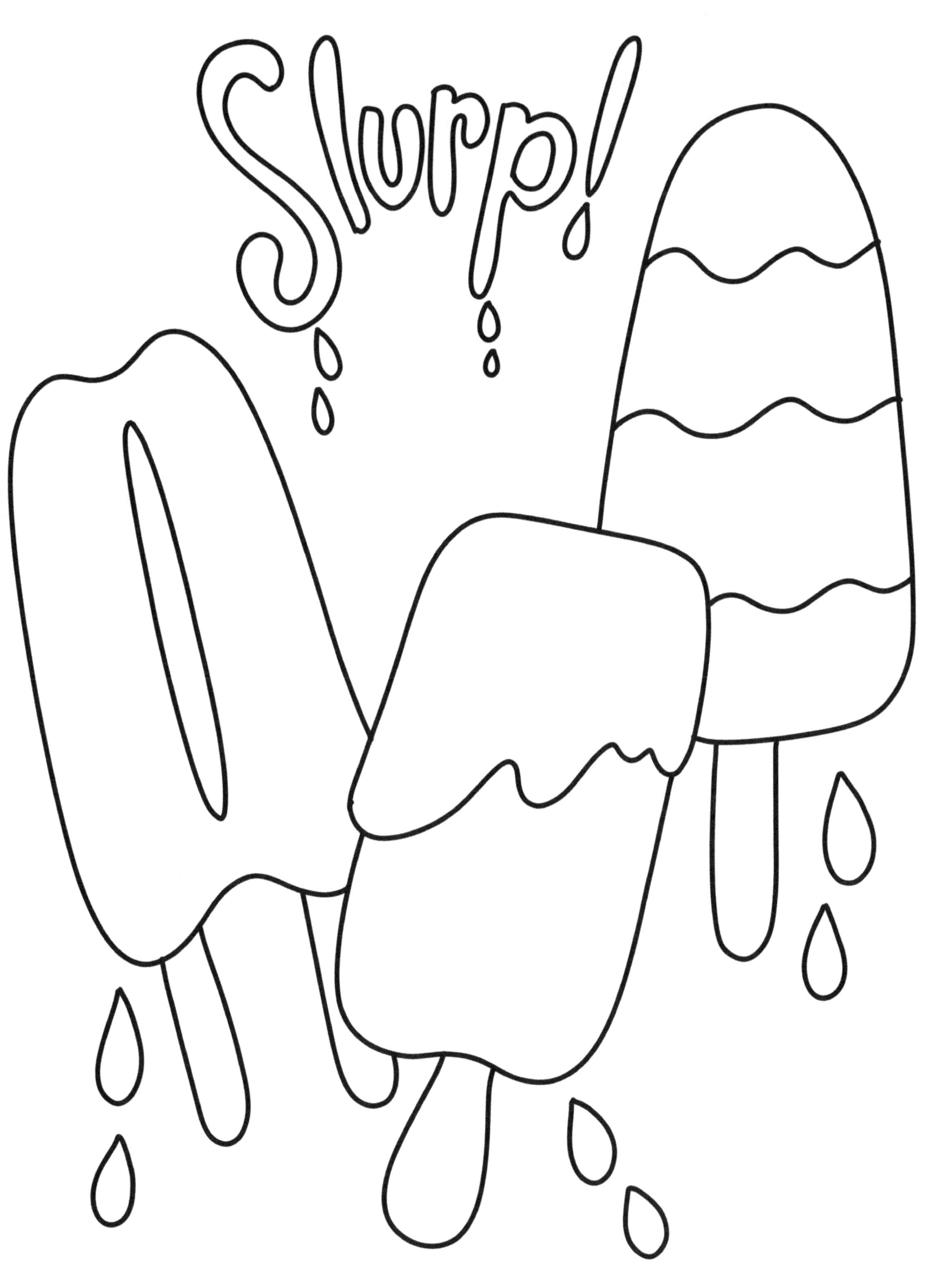
Slurp!

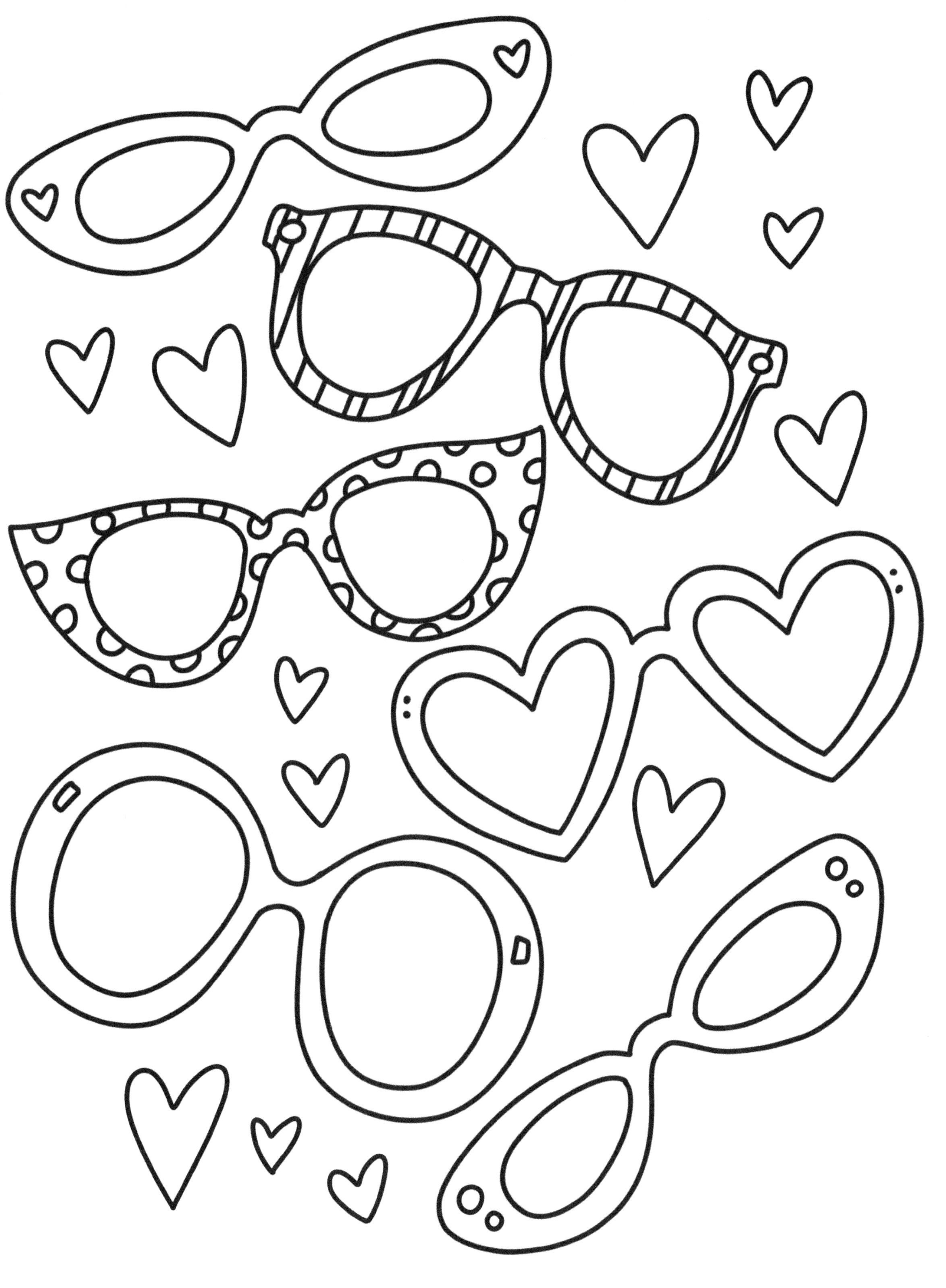

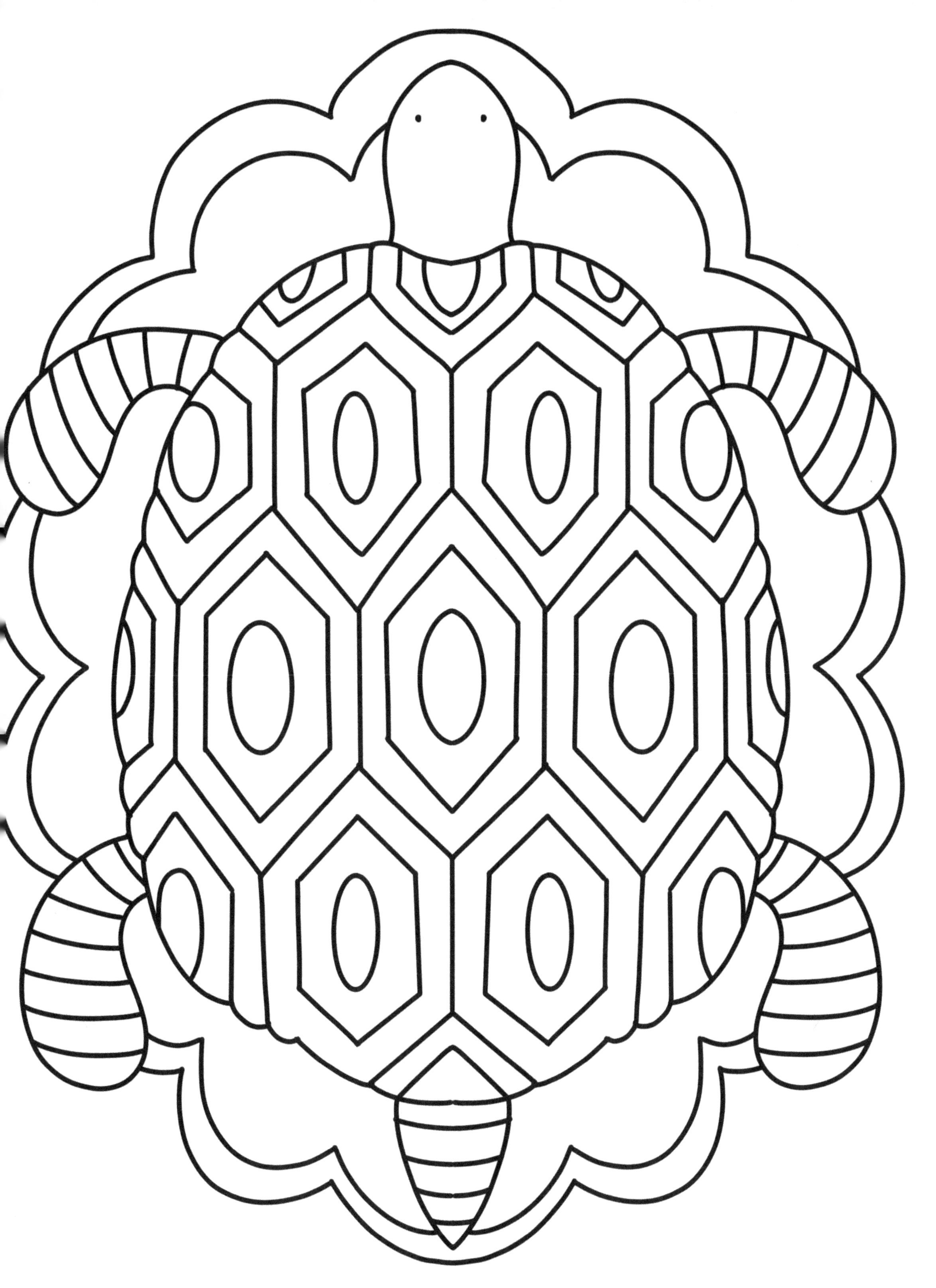

More books from The Coloring Café!

The Coloring Cafe-Volume One
The Coloring Cafe-Volume Two
The Coloring Cafe-To Go! A travel size coloring book!
The Coloring Cafe-Inspired Heart
The Coloring Cafe-Bible Blessings to Color
The Coloring Café-Stress Relief
The Coloring Café-Fashion Girls
The Coloring Café-Paper Dolls to Color
The Coloring Cafe-Coloring Christmas
The Coloring Cafe-Happy Times
The Coloring Cafe-You've Got This, Girl!
The Coloring Cafe-Everyday Angels
The Coloring Cafe-Affirmations
The Coloring Cafe-You Are Enough
The Coloring Cafe-Easy & Simple Everyday Large Print Coloring Book
The Coloring Cafe-Easy & Simple Mandalas Large Print Coloring Book
The Coloring Cafe-Easy & Simple Bible Verse Large Print Coloring Book
Cuppa Calm-An Inspirational Coloring Journal
Cuppa Cute-A Fashion Inspired Coloring Journal

Books for KIDS from The Coloring Café!

The Coloring Cafe-Colorful KIDS-AMAZING ME!
The Coloring Cafe-Colorful KIDS at Christmas
The Coloring Cafe-Happy Kids Color Christmas
The Coloring Cafe-Happy Kids Color Animals
The Coloring Cafe-Happy Kids Color Their World
The Coloring Cafe-Happy Kids Color Monsters

From CQ Publishing:

The Coloring Café-It's a Girl Thing
The Coloring Café-My Cup Runneth Over
The Coloring Café-Happy Everything
The Coloring Café- Kindness Matters
The Coloring Café-Relax, Unwind and Color
The Coloring Café-Life is Delicious
The Colorful Café-Colorful Blessings
The Coloring Cafe-Home is Where it All Begins
The Coloring Café-Be the Sunshine

About The Artist

Ronnie Walter is an artist and award winning writer. She licenses her illustrations on all kinds of products including stickers, greeting cards, stationery, giftware, fabric and more.

Besides the creator of The Coloring Cafe series of adult coloring books, Ronnie is the author of *License to Draw! How to Monetize your Art through Art Licensing...and more!* and *Gruesome Greetings, A Georgie Hardtman Mystery,* both available in paperback and Kindle.

Ronnie lives in paradise with her husband Jim Marcotte and the best shelter dog ever, Larry.

Email: coloringcafe@gmail.com
Facebook: Coloring Cafe
Instagram: @thecoloringcafe #thecoloringcafe
Twitter: @thecoloringcafe

www.thecoloringcafe.com

Test your colors here:

www.ingramcontent.com/pod-product-compliance
Lightning Source LLC
LaVergne TN
LVHW061253100826
845148LV00008B/1114
* 9 7 8 1 7 3 6 1 5 7 4 7 3 *